Exploring
NEW ORLEANS
A FAMILY GUIDE

Larenda Lyles Roberts

Seaside Press

Library of Congress Cataloging-in-Publication Data

Roberts, Larenda Lyles.
  Exploring New Orleans : a family guide / Larenda Lyles Roberts.
     p. cm.
  Includes index.
  ISBN 1-55622-620-9 (pbk.)
  1. New Orleans (La.)—Guidebooks. 2. Family recreation—
Louisiana—New Orleans—Guidebooks. I. Title.
  F379.N53R64   1998   98-22264
  917.63'350463—dc21   CIP

Seaside Press is an imprint of Wordware Publishing, Inc.
No part of this book may be reproduced in any form or by any means
without permission in writing from Wordware Publishing, Inc.

Printed in the United States of America

ISBN 1-55622-620-9
10 9 8 7 6 5 4 3 2 1
9807

All inquiries for volume purchases of this book should be addressed to
Wordware Publishing, Inc., at 2320 Los Rios Boulevard, Plano, Texas
75074. Telephone inquiries may be made by calling:

(972) 423-0090

Table of Contents

Contents

Contents

to Ellen Karnes

Acknowledgments

I wish to thank several people whose help made this book a reality. First of all, thanks to Mary Goldman and Dianne Stultz, my editors, for giving me this opportunity. I owe a special debt to my friend Charlotte Knipmeyer for sharing her knowledge and love of New Orleans with me. Her vast collection of newspaper clippings is unequaled in most libraries. I also wish to thank John McGill of the Williams Research Center, who helped me with the photographs of old New Orleans. I am grateful to Ann Lyles, my mother, and another wonderful cook, Joan Pearson, for supplying me with tasty recipes (and food!) for the book. Thanks also to Merle Shannon and my brother and sister-in-law, Bob and CeCe Lyles, for giving me tips to help in research.

New Orleans is a seductive town that gets into your blood and stays there. I grew up near New Orleans and have visited the city countless times. It is my hope that readers of this book will learn to love and appreciate the city as I have.

Test Your Knowledge

How much do you really know about New Orleans? Take the following test and find out.

1. How does one pronounce "Tchoupitoulas," as in Tchoupitoulas Street and the Wild Tchoupitoulas?
   A. Tic-how-pitolas.
   B. Tich-chew-pa-tolas.
   C. Chop-ah-two-lass.
   D. Shop-a-too-less.

2. Who or what was "Bronze John"?
   A. A statue of Pirate Jean Lafitte in Lafitte Park.
   B. A name given to the dreadful yellow fever epidemics that frequently swept through the city.
   C. An Indian guide who was a navigator for French explorer Bienville.

3. Who were the casket girls?
   A. A group of young girls who came from France to New Orleans in the 1700s with their belongings in a "casket" or trunk.
   B. A macabre Mardi Gras krewe that paraded during the 1920s.
   C. Women who decorated homes with funeral wreaths and black crepe following a death, according to French custom.

4. Why is June 23 an important date in New Orleans history?
   A. It marks St. Jude's Day, an important Catholic holiday.
   B. It is the date of the founding of New Orleans.
   C. It is St. John's Eve, an important date in the

practice of voodoo.

D. It is the date of the death of voodoo queen Marie Laveau.

5. What does it mean if you get a gold bean in your piece of king cake?
   A. You will be under a voodoo curse.
   B. The cook must practice voodoo.
   C. You must host the next Mardi Gras party.
   D. You will have to buy the next king cake.
   E. Both C and D.

6. Who were the Razzy Dazzy Spasm Boys?
   A. A world-renowned jazz group that traveled the globe.
   B. A marching band popular in the mid-1800s that played for jazz funerals.
   C. A raucous street band.
   D. The first jazz group to play at Preservation Hall.

7. Why are red beans and rice traditionally served on Mondays in New Orleans?
   A. Because Creoles believe it brings good luck.
   B. Because Monday is washday and homemakers need something easy to cook.
   C. Because African slaves brought the tradition with them.
   D. To celebrate deliverance from Spanish tyranny.

8. What is a banquette?
   A. An elaborate meal of gourmet French dishes.
   B. A piece of dining room furniture.
   C. A sidewalk.
   D. A deck on a riverboat.

9. What are the "Cities of the Dead"?
   A. A group of museums in Jackson Square.

B. Elaborate graveyards that date back to the 1700s.
C. Aboveground cemeteries.
D. Haunted places where vampires have been sighted.
E. Both B and C.

10. What should you never do in New Orleans?
    A. Walk down Bourbon Street at night.
    B. Call the city "New Orleens."
    C. Pet an alligator.
    D. Dip your beignets in your café-au-lait.

Answers

1. C
2. B
3. A
4. C
5. E
6. C
7. B
8. C
9. E
10. B

Red beans and rice is ready!

Shouted at the Royal Street Grocery
on Mondays

Uniquely New Orleans

The New Orleans Attitude and How to Develop It

Laissez les bon temps roulet. Let the good times roll. The City That Care Forgot. Old Man River. The Vieux Carré. Dining at Antoine's. Breakfast at Brennan's. Jazz at Tipitina's. The Garden District on a sultry summer evening. Café-au-lait and beignets at Café du Monde.

When you enter New Orleans, you enter another world—a world of gentility, lacy iron balconies dripping with ferns, narrow streets, hidden courtyards, and secret alleys. People aren't in a hurry in New Orleans. For one thing, it's too hot to exert oneself too much, and besides, the past is too interesting to ignore. Where else can you see cemeteries that look like miniature cities inviting you to come in and explore their rich history?

The New Orleans attitude is one of laid-back nonchalance. New Orleans citizens are casual, easygoing, and they love to have a good time. Parades, partying, and eating out are major parts of their lives. To blend in, it's necessary for a visitor to slow down and hang loose.

1

Lacy iron balconies in the French Quarter. *Photo by Grant L. Robertson*

So how do you blend in if you're in town from a faraway place—like New York City—to have a good time? Wear light cottons in summer and light wool in winter. Carry an umbrella during the summer, because fierce afternoon thunderstorms regularly blow in from the Gulf of Mexico. Stroll and smile—New Orleanians are friendly and usually greet passers by on the banquettes (that's the word used for "sidewalk"). You'll need comfortable shoes and a good pair of sunglasses for the brilliant sunshine. Even though summer heat is harsh, it's a good idea to take a light jacket, because many restaurants are overly air-conditioned.

Uptown, Downtown, and All Around

Due to the way New Orleans is situated on a curve of the Mississippi River, it's difficult to tell which way is north, south, east, or west. So instead of getting out a compass, the natives refer to "Uptown," which is the area north of Canal Street and "Downtown," which is, loosely speaking, south of Canal. Canal Street is the dividing line of the city, and streets on the northern side are prefixed "North," while those on the other side are "South." "Lakeside" is towards Lake Pontchartrain, and "Riverside" means near the Mississippi River.

So forget your conventional directions and reorient yourself to Uptown, Downtown, Lakeside, and Riverside. If you get lost, there is usually someone around who is willing to help out.

Relax, hang loose, and get ready to have a good time!

N'Yawlins Speakeasy
A Glossary for Yankees and Other Visitors

beignet (been-yay)—a French doughnut (without the hole) that is deep-fried and doused with powdered sugar. Goes with your café-au-lait.

café-au-lait—coffee with chicory and steamed milk; this popular drink made the Café du Monde famous.

chicory—a root that is roasted, ground, and then added to coffee to flavor it.

crawfish (cra<u>w</u>-fish)—also called "mudbugs" and "tiny lobsters," these famous shellfish are delicious fried, cooked in gumbo or jambalaya, or eaten straight out of the shell. The locals know to suck the heads of the little creatures after consumption to get the extra flavor out.

etouffée (ay-too-fay)—(means "smothered") a crawfish or shrimp dish made with a roux, onions, bell peppers, celery, and spices in a rich seafood broth. Served over rice.

filé—ground sassafras leaves used in flavoring gumbo; inspired by Choctaw Indians.

gumbo—from the African word for okra, "kingombo." A Cajun or Creole roux-based soup with seafood, chicken, and/or sausage added; usually served over rice. Okra is often used in seasoning gumbo, along with filé, which consists of ground sassafras leaves.

jambalaya (jam-ba-lie-ya)—a spicy dirty rice dish made with seafood, chicken, sausage, onion, bell pepper, and whatever else the Creole cook has left in the refrigerator at the end of the week.

lagniappe (lan-yap)—from French *la nappe*; translated "a little something extra." Originated when storekeepers would give children a licorice or treat; now means anything given freely.

muffuletta—a round Italian sandwich that originated in New Orleans and consists of meats, cheese, an Italian olive sauce, plus about anything else you want on it.

New Orleans (N'Yawlins, New Orlunz, or New Or-lee-unz)—NEVER NEW ORLEENS! This is the most common mistake visitors make in the Crescent City. When locals hear you say "New Orleens," they snicker and shake their heads behind your back. It is an understandable mistake, however, since many songs pronounce N'Yawlins "New Orleens," and the word "Orleans" alone, as in Orleans Parish, is pronounced "Orleens."

po-boy sandwich—This stuffed wonder originated in New Orleans as "poor boy sandwiches." Served on French bread, po-boys are usually stuffed with fried oysters or shrimp, ham, and other meats. A "dressed" po-boy is served with lettuce, tomato, and mayonnaise. "Undressed" is a plain po-boy. A purist eating a fried oyster po-boy will have nothing but butter and fried oysters on it.

praline (praw-leen)—a caramelized sugar and pecan Creole confection. Sold in most food stores and a great pick-me-up for the afternoon blood sugar low.

roux (roo)—a dark brown sauce made from flour and oil; the darker the better. "First you make a roux," is a classic phrase from Creole recipes.

> *New Orleans food is as delicious as the less criminal forms of sin.*
>
> Mark Twain, 1884

Food and Fun

Once you get a taste of New Orleans food, you are spoiled for life. Not only is New Orleans America's favorite food city, it is renowned internationally for the unique blend of Creole and Cajun cuisine. Creole dishes are generally of French and Spanish origin, with African cooking thrown in for spice, while Cajun food is hotter and heartier fare. When you visit New Orleans, come prepared to eat! New Orleans visitors generally abandon calorie counting and cholesterol tables in exchange for the shrimp Creole, crawfish etouffée, and the delicious seafood gumbo.

As early New Orleans grew, European, African, and West Indies people came there, each culture adapting their native dishes to blend with the bountiful wild game and seafood in the woods and bayous surrounding the little settlement. Bouillabaisse, a "fish soup" that originated in the Provençe region of France, evolved into gumbo. Paella, a Spanish rice dish with vegetables and meat, became jambalaya, a spicy Cajun dish made with rice, seafood, and sausage.

German settlers introduced the skill of sausage making and charcuterie, or pig roasting. Native Americans showed the newcomers how to use spices such as filé powder (ground leaves of the sassafrass tree) to season gumbo and also to use bay leaves from laurel trees. The Africans brought their native okra with them, which is used to flavor gumbo. Governor Bienville opened the first cooking school in America. It was operated by Madame Langlois, the governor's housekeeper, who taught Creole wives how to use native foods and spices.

When you make gumbo or many of the other flavorful Creole and Cajun dishes, you must start by making a roux, which consists of equal parts flour and shortening cooked over medium to high heat until it becomes a thick brown sauce. The roux is then used as a base for the main dish, and the cook adds vegetables, stock, seafood, meat, and seasonings. Famed New Orleans Chef Paul Prudhomme refers to his roux as "Cajun napalm" because it can be dangerous to cook this mixture over high heat.

In New Orleans, cooking and eating are one of the favorite forms of entertainment. Visitors are impressed not only by the unique cuisine, but also by the number of small restaurants with their starched white tablecloths, crystal and silver, and attentive waiters. It is easy to have a gourmet meal for a reasonable price in New Orleans because of its abundance of dining establishments. There are plenty of famous restaurants, such as Antoine's, Arnaud's, Brennan's, Commander's Palace, and K-Paul's. If you have time to explore, look for the small cafés such as The Gumbo Shop on St. Peter's that serve great food as well.

One could write for hours about food, but if you want to really get a taste of New Orleans in your home, try one of the following authentic New Orleans recipes. Remember to use only the freshest or fresh-frozen seafood. Crawfish and shrimp, while still not easily found in many areas, are much more readily available than in the past, because they are now being harvested and marketed outside Louisiana. So get your apron and cooking utensils out, and dig in. *C'est ci bon!*

Hot Crab Dip

1 stick butter
6 green onions, chopped
¼ cup parsley, chopped
3 tblsp. flour
2 cups half and half cream

cayenne pepper & salt to taste
¾ lb. grated Swiss cheese
2 tblsp. sherry
1 lb. fresh or frozen white crab meat

Sauté onions and parsley in butter. Blend in flour, cream, and cheese until cheese melts. Add other ingredients and fold in crabmeat. Serve hot or in chafing dish with toasted round crackers.

Creole Seasoning

2 tblsp. onion powder
2 tblsp. oregano
1 tblsp. thyme
1 tblsp. cayenne pepper

2 tblsp. garlic powder
2 tblsp. basil
1 tblsp. white pepper
5 tblsp. paprika

May be used to season meat or fish.

Beignets

1 pkg. dry yeast	7 cups all purpose flour
1½ cups warm water	¼ cup shortening
½ cup sugar	vegetable oil
2 eggs	powdered sugar
1 cup evaporated milk	

In a large bowl, sprinkle yeast over water; stir to dissolve. Add sugar, salt, eggs, and milk. Blend in mixer. Add 4 cups of the flour and beat smooth. Add shortening; beat in remaining flour. Cover with plastic wrap and chill overnight. Roll out on floured board to ¼" thickness. Cut into 2 x 2" squares. Deep fry at 360 degrees until lightly browned on each side. Drain on paper towels and sprinkle with powdered sugar. Dough will keep in refrigerator several days. Dough may be frozen. Cut doughnuts and then freeze. Thaw and fry.

Noel Shrimp Bake

Cook in ¼ cup margarine:	Add:
½ cup chopped celery	2 cups cooked shrimp
1 cup chopped onion	1 tsp. salt
1 cup chopped green pepper	½ stick butter or margarine
	2 cups cooked rice
	½ tsp. chili powder
	Tabasco to taste

Bake at 350 degrees 50-60 minutes. Garnish with chopped parsley. This is a change from traditional shrimp Creole that is served over rice, but it makes a festive and easy party dish.

Crawfish Etouffée

3 medium onions, chopped	½ cup bell pepper, chopped
½ cup celery, chopped	2 tblsp. flour
3 tblsp. oil	4 lb. crawfish tails
2 tblsp. parsley, chopped	2 tblsp. green onion,
salt & pepper to taste	chopped

9

In iron skillet add oil and flour; make light roux. Let roux cool a few minutes and then add seasonings. Smother 10 or 15 minutes. Add crawfish tails and ½ cup water. Cook 15-20 minutes. Add green onion and parsley. If mixture is too thick, add more water. Serve over rice.

Seafood Gumbo

1 lb. lean bacon, chopped
1 cup flour
1 stalk celery, chopped
3 or 4 lbs. onions, chopped
½ green pepper, chopped
6 cloves garlic, crushed
1 to 1½ lbs. okra, sliced (may use frozen)
6 cups water
2 (14 ½ oz.) cans whole tomatoes, chopped
salt & pepper to taste
cayenne pepper to taste
2 (14½ oz.) cans chicken broth
4 cups water
1 lb. crabmeat
3 lbs. shrimp
½ cup sliced andouille sausage
1 (6 oz.) can Contadina tomato paste

Fry bacon in large heavy pot; remove bacon and crumble. Make a roux by stirring flour into bacon fat; cook over very low heat until roux is dark brown, 30 to 40 minutes. Do not burn, stir often. Add chopped vegetables, garlic, tomatoes, tomato sauce, water, and chicken broth. Cook 30 minutes. Add sausage and crabmeat, then salt, black pepper, and cayenne pepper. Add half of the shrimp. Cook about an hour, and add remaining shrimp and crumbled bacon. Cook 15 minutes. Add filé the last 5 minutes of cooking time. Adjust seasoning to taste.

New Orleans Style Red Beans and Rice

1 lb. kidney beans, washed and drained
1 lb. med. or hot link sausage, cut in 1" slices
salt to taste
1 large onion, chopped
1 clove garlic, minced
2 bay leaves
6 cups water
1 tsp. sugar

Soak beans several hours or overnight in cold water. Drain and put in fresh water, add onion, garlic, bay leaves, and sausage. Cook slowly for 1½ to 2 hours until gravy is thick and dark. Add salt, pepper, and sugar the last ½ hour of cooking. Serve on mounds of cooked rice.

Louisiana Sweet Potato Soufflé

3 cups mashed cooked sweet potatoes
2 eggs

½ cup sugar
½ tsp. salt

Mix together and add:
½ stick margarine
⅓ cup milk

½ tsp. vanilla
½ tsp. cinnamon

Topping:
1 cup brown sugar
1 cup nuts

⅓ stick margarine
⅓ cup flour

Place on top and bake at 350 degrees for 35 minutes.

Pralines

2½ cups sugar
⅔ cup evaporated milk

¾ stick butter
2 cups pecans

Put 2 cups sugar, butter, and milk in one (heavy) pot. Put remaining ½ cup sugar in a dry (heavy) pot. Place both pots on medium heat at same time. Keep stirring the ½ cup sugar and when melted add to the other pot. Cook the combined mixture until it reaches the soft ball stage. Add the pecans. Beat until thick. Test by dropping a small amount on wax paper. If this holds its form, then drop tablespoon sized amounts (or larger) on wax paper, leaving some space between each praline. Let cool and gently slide them off.

Favorite Restaurants

The following restaurants are only a few of the delicious dining establishments in New Orleans.

Antoine's—One of the city's better-known restaurants; famous for oyster dishes; expensive. 713 St. Louis St. 581-4422.

Arnaud's—Famous French Quarter restaurant; known for Shrimp Arnaud; expensive. 813 Bienville St. 581-5433.

Brennan's—This restaurant originated Bananas Foster; also famous for "Breakfast at Brennan's"; expensive. 417 Royal St. 525-9711.

Camellia Grill—Known for burgers and pastries; an extremely popular lunch spot. 626 S. Carrollton Ave. 866-9573.

Commander's Palace—Jazz brunch is popular; excellent Creole dishes; expensive. 1427 Washington Ave. 899-8221.

Emeril's—Home of Chef Emeril Lagasse; nouvelle and traditional cuisine. 800 Tchoupitoulas St. 528-9393.

Galatoire's—Exquisite Creole cuisine; a New Orleans institution; expensive. 209 Bourbon St. 525-2021.

Gumbo Shop—Delicious authentic gumbo and other Creole dishes; reasonable prices. 630 St. Peter St. 525-1486.

K-Paul's Louisiana Kitchen—Famed Chef Paul Prudhomme's place is popular for classic Creole and Cajun food; delicious and reasonable luncheon dishes; moderately expensive; no reservations. 416 Chartres St. 524-7394.

Mother's—Known for po-boys and fried seafood; opens early for breakfast. 401 Poydras. 523-9656.

Praline Connection II Gospel & Blues Hall—Famous for Sunday jazz brunch featuring jazz and gospel; moderate prices. 901-907 S. Peters. 523-3972.

Cities of the Dead

Some of the most famous sites in New Orleans are its cemeteries, christened "Cities of the Dead" by a writer visiting in
the mid-1800s. These fascinating cities within a city consist of
rows and rows of narrow, raised tombs that resemble doll-
houses of brick, stucco, or marble. Some aboveground graves
have miniature ornamental iron "galleries" and iron gates
with garden chairs and benches, resulting in the effect that
the interred body is receiving guests.

Cities of the Dead. The unusual and unique burial vaults are all aboveground
to escape intrusion by the high water table. *Photo by Grant L. Robertson*

Floating Coffins

The reason for these architectural wonders is the fact that New Orleans lies some four to six feet below sea level. In earlier times, before the city's powerful pumping and drainage system was in place, a six-foot hole would quickly become filled with 5'11" of water and mud, causing the casket to rise back up. Gravediggers were often forced to immerse floating coffins using long wooden poles. The distaste of settling a "gurgling" coffin was sometimes overcome by large holes bored through the bottom, allowing water to enter and quickly sink the coffin.

This problem, along with a fear that unsanitary conditions were responsible for growing epidemics of yellow fever and cholera, led city officials in the early 1800s to order that all interments be aboveground. The law gave rise to what a delighted Mark Twain called "the only real architecture in New Orleans." Some graves were simple whitewashed "ovens"; others were elaborate Greek Revival structures with pillared entranceways, gables, and even stained-glass windows. Marble cherubs, weeping widows, and mystic Egyptian figures adorn tombs, which take on a life of their own and make visitors feel a sense of welcome and serenity. Walking through the Cities of the Dead can be a pleasant excursion through New Orleans' diverse culture. (See note below*.) Many structures contain several generations of family members, because the law permits multiple burials on each site. After the first burial, when subsequent family members die, the coffin is removed and the bones are pushed to the back to make room for the next body.

---

* Readers are cautioned NOT to visit cemeteries unless on an organized tour.

Pirates and Voodoo Queens

St. Louis No. 1*, located just outside the French Quarter and one of New Orleans' oldest cemeteries, contains the remains of early residents, including the two voodoo queens, Marie Laveau I and II, and chess champion Paul Morphy. French soldier-turned-pirate Dominique You is buried in St. Louis No. 1 as well. After proving himself in the Battle of New Orleans in 1815, You decided to become a pirate with Jean Lafitte's band. In later years, he returned to a reasonably honest life as a ward politician, causing distress to many townspeople who had romanticized Dominique You's adventurous life. You died an obscure pauper, but upon learning of his demise, New Orleans remembered him, closing stores and firing military guns for his funeral.

The Voodoo Queen's Grave

The tomb of at least one of the Marie Laveaus (there were two: mother and daughter) is found in St. Louis No. 1, marked by dozens of red crosses, which followers of the voodoo queen have scratched into the whitewashed structure, in hopes that Marie will grant their wishes. The inscription reads, "MARIE PHILOMÉNE GLAPION, FAMILLE VVE. PARIS née LAVEAU, Ci-Git, décédée, le 11 juin 1897." This is the flamboyant daughter of the first Marie Laveau, who married a cabinetmaker named Glapion during the 1820s. According to the oldest sources, Marie I's remains rest in the bottom of the three-tiered "oven" in St. Louis No. 1.

St. Louis No. 2, however, claims that it has the remains of Marie II, as do numerous other cemeteries around town. In earlier times, when the cemeteries were relatively safe places (St. Louis No. 1 is very dangerous), visitors left coins, soft drinks, roasted chickens with oyster dressing, and even fresh chocolate cakes for the voodoo queen. In fact, caretakers told followers that Marie's remains had been moved because so many were showing up "prayin' and hollerin', huntin' luck," thus giving rise to the confusion of her resting place.

St. Louis No. 2 Cemetery is located on N. Claiborne Avenue, and St. Louis No. 3 is further out near Bayou St. John along Esplanade Avenue. In the old days, New Orleans bluebloods bragged about their places in these cemeteries. Today, the older cemeteries can be dangerous; in fact, St. Louis No. 1 is so bad that tours conducted by Save Our Cemeteries, a preservation group, are accompanied by a New Orleans police officer. Readers are cautioned not to visit St. Louis No. 1 or No. 2 except with an organized tour.

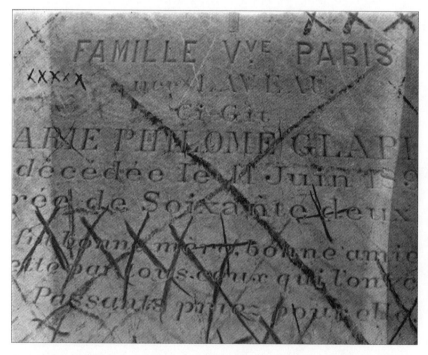

Crosses superimposed on supposed tomb of Marie Laveau by superstitious persons. *Historic New Orleans Collection.*

Faith, Hope, Love, and Mrs. Moriarty

The largest privately owned monument in town, and possibly the United States, may be seen from Interstate 10 when crossing the Metairie Road overpass in Metairie Cemetery. It was once a racetrack and also a favorite among New Orleans' old families. The 85-foot granite structure topped with a cross was commissioned by Irish immigrant and New Orleans businessman Daniel Moriarty, for his wife, Mary, who died in 1887.

It seems that Mrs. Moriarty, who was much older than her husband, was snubbed by New Orleans society during her lifetime, and Daniel decided to build an overpowering memorial so that his wife would be able to look down her nose at everyone else from her grave. The cross itself was designed to be large enough for a man to stand under its arm. Daniel ordered the sculptor to erect statues of the four virtues. When informed that there were only three virtues—Faith, Hope, and Charity—he insisted there be four anyway. Locals dubbed the four prodigious ladies they built "Faith, Hope, Charity, and Mrs. Moriarty." A special railroad track had to be laid to transport the granite "virtues" to their positions. The massive monument cost $185,000, very little of which was ever paid.

The Knocking Maiden

Another well-known tomb in the Metairie Cemetery is the former resting place of famous Storyville madam Josie Arlington. Miss Arlington died in 1914 and was laid to rest in a pink marble tomb in the cemetery that she had built for $15,000. The Grecian-type structure boasted a copper door, two flambeaux (flaming torches), stone urns, and the figure of a young maiden leaning forward as if to knock on the imposing door. Some said the girl represented Josie on the night she stayed out too late and was refused admittance by her father, an incident that eventually led to her life of prostitution. Others said the girl symbolized Josie's house rule—no virgins admitted.

At any rate, Miss Arlington was laid to rest in the big pink tomb. Several years later, a traffic signal was erected on the street just outside the cemetery, causing the two flambeaux to glow red at night and give the illusion of a red light shining in the madam's tomb. This spectacle brought crowds who gathered each evening to watch the "red-light" grave come to life. The city eventually replaced the red light with a white one, and around 1924 Miss Arlington's niece sold the tomb and had her aunt's bones transferred to a receiving vault. Today the Morales family owns the monument. The famous Storyville madam's name has been removed, but the young girl still leans to knock on the copper door, and locals say the large tomb continues to glow red on occasion.

St. Roch's and Blood-Spotted Clovers

Many other Cities of the Dead exist in New Orleans, including Lafayette Nos. 1 and 2, used for many of the yellow fever victims. Benevolent societies, formed beginning in the late 1700s, often provided burial sites for their members, usually blacks or other groups of a common ethnic origin. St. Roch Cemetery, for example, was opened in 1868 to serve Italian immigrants.

Located at St. Roch and Derbigny Streets, St. Roch is considered one of the quaintest of New Orleans' cemeteries. It is modeled after the famous Campo Santo dei Tedeschi (Holy Field of the Germans) near St. Peter's in Rome. A German priest, Father Thevis, came to New Orleans in the 1800s as assistant pastor to the Holy Trinity Church. A terrible yellow fever epidemic in 1868 confronted the young priest, who asked St. Roch's intercession in sparing his congregation. St.

Roch was known for his work with plague sufferers in the Middle Ages. Father Thevis promised to erect a chapel to St. Roch with his own hands. The congregation was spared, and Father Thevis went to work, building a small chapel of brick-covered cement, with tall narrow windows and a small carved wood altar with a statue of St. Roch and his faithful dog. On each side of the altar, along the walls, are marble emblems and plaques, along with artificial limbs and crutches put there as testimony to the cures attributed to the saint. Father Thevis is buried under the floor.

For many years on each Good Friday, young Catholic girls made a pilgrimage to St. Roch's Chapel because of a local legend promising a husband to those who said a prayer and left a small sum of money at nine different churches. It was said that ending the pilgrimage at St. Roch's was doubly lucky if the girl picked a four-leaf clover in the old cemetery yard. The red-spotted clovers of St. Roch's were said to be from blood spatters of a young bride-to-be who committed suicide on her lover's grave.

All Saints' Day

On the first day of November every year, the cemeteries come alive with families and friends showing up to clean, scrub, whitewash, and decorate the graves of their loved ones in celebration of All Saints' Day. This citywide observance is an old European tradition and reflects New Orleanians' devotion to their deceased loved ones. In times past, many stores and businesses closed and turned out for the event.

Women appear at the burial grounds with flowers (usually bright purple or yellow chrysanthemums) and wreaths, mops, paintbrushes, and food. All Saints' Day is a family affair, and people meet at the cemeteries not only to clean, but to gossip and visit with friends they haven't seen for a year. Sometimes the grave of a stranger is cleaned as well and a few flowers placed on it.

The people of New Orleans are famous for their devotion to saints, which takes many forms. One needs only to look in the classified section of the *Times Picayune* to see the many ads placed daily thanking various saints for prayers answered. Sometimes there is a "run" on one saint when word gets out that he or she has granted favors.

Married or Buried

Some people are *really* fascinated by the Cities of the Dead, as was a Neiman Marcus executive from Houston who chose one of the Lafayette cemeteries for his wedding. The event took place on Friday the 13th on an aisle of the cemetery to the tune of "Summertime," played by a lone trumpet. Bride, groom, and guests all wore black, and the graveyard superintendent was told that both bride and groom had been married before and wanted to bury their pasts and get married at the same time.

You might not want to get married or buried in New Orleans, but a visit to its famous aboveground cemeteries are part of the spiritual New Orleans experience.

Save Our Cemeteries, Inc.
(504) 588-9357
Lafayette No. 1, St. Louis
No. 1—all profits used to
restore cemeteries.

Gray Line Tours
2 Canal St. Ste. 1300
(504) 587-0709; 800-535-7786

St. Louis No. 3, Lafayette
Cukie's Travels Inc.
61171 Brittany Dr.
LaCombe, LA 70445
Two- and three-hour
walking and riding tours.
(504) 882-3058

Jazz and Other Forms of Musical Expression
—*From the Razzy Dazzy Spasm Boys to the Jazz & Heritage Festival*

From primitive vibrations of pebble-filled gourds in Congo Square to the blue notes of a lone street trumpeter, the people of New Orleans have always found forms of music to express themselves. The music that permeates the streets of New Orleans today came from the rhythm of African jungles, the richness of the West Indies, and the heat-filled Louisiana swamps alive with night sounds.

Congo Square

As early as the late 1700s, free Negroes held citywide balls that drew freemen and slaves alike from all over the area. Blacks also congregated at Congo Square (now Louis Armstrong Park), where they practiced native African rituals and danced traditional tribal dances. Slaves gathered at Congo Square every Sunday with fiddles, tambourines, and banjoes to play their unique music borne of trauma, suffering, and the *joie de vivre* that kept them going.

Visitors and residents also gathered to watch the slaves "dance Congo," a colorful and exotic ritual of "weaving and stomping under the sycamore-trees," as one writer described it. Favorite dances included the Calenda, a form of which was used in voodoo ceremonies, and the Bamboula. Both were based on ancient African dances, with a touch of French movement thrown in.

A City Filled With Music

Many free Negroes of New Orleans were given music lessons by French, German, and Italian musicians, who were numerous in the city. In the late 1830s a Negro Philharmonic Society with over one hundred members existed in New Orleans. By the time of the Civil War (1861-1865), black musicians played for brothels, dances, marching bands, and an occasional theater. Many of the brothels employed black "professors" (as they were called) to play the piano, and the really fancy houses boasted of orchestras.

In New Orleans' early years, music was primarily from the opera and local orchestras. By 1840, when the population was around 103,000, close to one thousand pianos had already entered the city. From 1831 to 1841 there were twenty-six stores in the city that handled music, twenty-one of which dealt in music exclusively. For many years during the nineteenth century, New Orleans was the only American city with a resident opera company.

There were also groups of itinerant musicians who played in the streets and saloons for coins. Most were former slaves who captured the jungle beat and improvised with iron kettles, gas pipes, cigar boxes, and anything they could find to use for an instrument.

Birth of Jazz

Jazz was born from these street musicians who entertained New Orleans with their strange, raucous sounds. One of the earliest of these groups was the Razzy Dazzy Spasm Band, whom some credit as being the original jazz band. Although that statement is arguable, there is no doubt that the group of seven boys, aged twelve to fifteen years, were instrumental in bringing the new sound to the forefront.

The word "jass," as the music was first called, means "fornicate" and comes from an old English word that may be found in Shakespeare and Chaucer. Harry Gregson was the manager and singer of the Razzy Dazzy Spasm Band. Gregson couldn't afford a megaphone, so he improvised with a piece of gas pipe. The others in the group were Willie Bussey, known as Cajun, who played the harmonica, Emile Lacomb (Stalebread Charley) on a fiddle fashioned out of a cigar box, Charley Stein on the kettle, and Chinee, Emile Benrod (Whiskey), Frank Bussey (Monk), and Warm Gravy on the horns and whistles. Stein also used a gourd filled with pebbles and a cowbell. In later life he became a famous drummer. The real names of Chinee and Warm Gravy are not known.

This clever and colorful group entertained New Orleans with their jazzy melodies and street antics, often standing on their heads, going into contortions, and interrupting the music with melancholy howls of "hi-de-hi" and "ho-de-ho." One author notes that such expressions, which he calls "the exclusive howls of Negro bandleaders," were used a hundred years earlier in Mississippi River songs.

Spasm Bands

The Spasm band played in front of saloons and theaters and in the Storyville houses. Eventually they had a few formal engagements at the Grand Opera House and other theaters, where they were billed as "The Razzy Dazzy Spasm Band." One of their biggest moments came when they played for actress Sarah Bernhardt, who was amazed at their talent and unique sound. It wasn't long before spasm bands sprang up all over the city, imitating the shaking, sawing upbeat tempo of the original Razzy Dazzy Spasm Band.

These spasm bands played various interpretations of black folk music, brass band sounds, and French tunes—all with a

New Orleans flavor, of course. Some of the better known tunes included "Tiger Ray," "Basin Street Blues," and "Canal Street Blues." Since parades were popular in New Orleans, marching bands proliferated, particularly following the Civil War. In the 1870s two Negro bands, the St. Bernard Brass Band and Kelly's Band, kept New Orleans supplied "with the best of martial music." When President Garfield died in 1881 over a dozen black bands turned out for his funeral parade.

Spasm jazz band. *National Geographic, 1930.*

Jazz Funerals

The famous jazz funerals have long been a New Orleans tradition. It was said that in New Orleans, the parade was so much loved that it "became an end in itself for the Negro." The bands didn't really need an occasion to march, but simply wanted to play their music and have fun, eventually becoming less formal and acquiring more rhythm and swing.

Ultimately, the black bands took over the funeral parade custom. The processions to the grave were stately and slow with the playing of somber hymns. The return, however, was a good-time parade as the departed person entered heaven, and the hymns gave way to gospel songs and celebratory songs of joy ("When the Saints Go Marchin' In"). Some of the famous early black bands were the Excelsior Brass Band, the Onward, the Tuxedo, and the Eureka. All contributed to the new sound of jazz. Today, the tradition of jazz funeral parades continues in New Orleans. When news goes out that a jazz musician has died, people come from surrounding communities to watch the colorful procession of musicians, parasols, trumpets, clarinets, and drums.

Jazz Across America

America first got a taste of the jazz sound when the Original Dixieland Jazz Band of New Orleans, ironically, a white band, recorded the music in 1917. Jazz was a completely new sound in the music world—a rough, earthy sound that expressed the blues of living. It came from the hearts and souls of oppressed people who knew the secrets of spicing their lives with a devil-may-care attitude and an unquenchable thirst for pleasure. As long as music was playing, who couldn't smile?

Even though their music was called dirty, lowdown, and accused of provoking "downright nausea," the majority of listeners were enthralled with the colorful, uplifting tunes from deep down South in New Orleans, and it wasn't long before New Orleans and jazz were synonymous.

Early Jazz Musicians

While the Original Dixieland Jazz Band, led by Nick LaRocca, played Chicago, New York, and London, the old-time musicians continued to play New Orleans, where the streets and saloons were alive nightly with the raucous sound. Buddy Bolden was one of the first great jazz players with a band. Known for his showmanship, Bolden usually traveled with three women. Another of the early jazz musician greats was Joseph "King" Oliver, born in 1885, who got his start touring with a boys' brass band on a steamboat to Baton Rouge. Soon he was playing horn with bands in Storyville joints. One night King Oliver walked out onto the street blowing in B-flat, and

Preservation Hall Jazz Band. Willie Humphrey on clarinet and Percy Humphrey on trumpet. *Historic New Orleans Collection*

everyone stopped to listen. It wasn't long before Oliver had his own band at Lala's Café, eventually going to Chicago and making the first big Negro recordings in 1922 as King Oliver's Creole Jazz Band.

Jelly Roll Morton (Ferdinand Joseph LaMothe, 1890-1941), a jazz pioneer who got his start playing piano in the brothels of Storyville, was a composer and Creole of color who credited himself with the creation of jazz. Jelly Roll entertained audiences with such numbers as "Honky Tonk Blues," "Kansas City Stomp," and "Darktown Strutters' Ball." After learning the piano and absorbing New Orleans culture, he became a part-time pool hustler and worked in vaudeville. Morton, who sported a diamond in his front tooth, also enjoyed success as a published composer and recording musician-pianist who traveled to New York and Chicago.

Low Down Blues

I can sit right here and think a thousand miles away,
Sit right here and think a thousand miles away,
Have the blues, I cannot remember the day.

Tell me, babe, what's on your mind,
Tell me, baby, what's on your dog-gone mind,
Tell me, baby, what's on your dog-gone mind.

I never b'lieved in havin' no one woman at a time,
Never b'lieved in havin' one woman at a time,
I always had six, seven, eight or nine.

I said, babe, oh, ba-by, babe,
Oh, babe, oh, ba-by,
You've got to set your Papa cra-zy.

I got a sweet woman, she lives right back of the jail,
I got a sweet woman lives right back of the jail,
She's got a sign on the window,
"Good Cabbage For Sale."

Jelly Roll Morton's style of heavy blues singing accompanied by elegant piano playing reflects his sporting-house background. Some of the lyrics were so raunchy they were not recorded until much later in his life. Jail, woman troubles, traveling, and honky-tonk life were all popular subjects for his songs.

Morton moved to Washington, D.C. in 1935, where Alan Lomax, a Library of Congress employee, heard him play and persuaded the singer to record a series of interviews and performances. Produced in 1938, the recordings are a remarkable account of the early history of jazz. They were reissued in 1993 by Rounder Records Corp. and are widely available on CD.

Some of the other early musicians of the time included Spencer Williams, Edward "Kid" Ory, and Sidney Bechet. A young kid hung around the street bands during this era, playing a four-string guitar with a flat-wood neck and cigarbox body, imitating their sounds and peddling coal for a living. A player gave the aspiring musician a used cornet one day, and the kid cut notches in the instrument to keep it firmly against his lips. He toughened his mouth and learned how to read a little music, but mostly he blew his cornet. His name was Louis Armstrong.

Louis Armstrong

Armstrong, born in 1901, began playing in Gravier Street dives for a dollar a night, eventually going on the riverboats with Fate Marable's Jazz-E-Saz Band. He got fifty dollars for his rights to "I Wish That I Could Shimmy Like My Sister Kate." After Storyville closed in 1917, Louis received a telegram from King Oliver in Chicago inviting him to come up and join the band. Armstrong joined King Oliver's band at the age of 22 and soon became a star in his own right.

"Satchmo," as he was called, is perhaps best known for his lively rendition of "Hello, Dolly." He spent much of the rest of his life traveling and performing around the world, only returning to New Orleans on rare occasions. Louis Armstrong, whose performances and recordings brought jazz into theaters all over the world, died in 1971.

May O'Brian's brothel in Storyville, c. 1934. *Historic New Orleans Collection*

Jazz Decline and Rise

With so many jazz greats leaving New Orleans, jazz experienced a period of decline in the 1940s and '50s, as rhythm and blues gained popularity in the music world. When Preservation Hall opened in 1961 at 726 St. Peter, newspapers wrote, "This may be its swan song." Three years later, an article in *The Richmond Dispatch* noted, "Jazz—the original New Orleans article—is on its deathbed." Fortunately for music and fun lovers everywhere, the ramshackle building featuring such greats as Percy and Willie Humphrey, Greg Stafford, Wendell Brunious, Dr. Michael White, Wynton Marsalis, and countless others, continued to play their music with dignity, love, and soul.

In 1964, when the Beatles were making music history, an instrumental recording by trumpeter Al Hirt, "Java," was making its way up the charts as well. The New Orleans native and son of a New Orleans policeman, teamed up with another native, Pete Fountain, in 1955, putting together a six-piece combo with the clarinet player. The two soon went solo, but their impact on music was felt around the world. Although the purists decried their labels as "jazz" musicians, the two were very successful commercially. Pete Fountain lives today with his wife Beverly just outside of New Orleans. Al "Jumbo" Hirt's career was jeopardized in 1970 when a brick hit him in the mouth as he stood on a float during a Mardi Gras parade. The injury resulted in stitches all across his lip. Hirt recovered, although he played fewer engagements and eventually closed his club on Bourbon Street. Today he still entertains New Orleanians at such events as the annual JazzFest.

As jazz spread around the globe, it continued to thrive on the hot steamy streets of New Orleans. Today music is heard everywhere in the Quarter, from ragtime piano notes sifting through enclosed courtyards to the old-time musicians warming up at Preservation Hall with the door propped open.

Annual Jazz and Heritage Festival

The annual New Orleans Jazz and Heritage Festival (JazzFest), which takes place the last weekend in April through the first weekend in May, promotes the gospel of New Orleans music to followers who come from just about everywhere. The JazzFest extravaganza is a ten-day affair, and it features not only the best of jazz, Cajun zydeco, R&B artists, and gospel choirs, but also fine Cajun cooking to heat the palates of hungry festival-goers. Held at the Fair Grounds Racetrack, the festival attracts several hundred thousand music lovers, who come with rain gear and sunscreen to hear such music greats as Aaron Neville, Jimmy Buffett, Dr. John (named after a voodoo priest), gospel choirs, and Cajun zydeco artists. The zydeco sound comes from French-speaking Acadians of southwest Louisiana and features a folksy, two-step rhythm played on keyboard and button accordion, fiddle, rub board, and triangle. Afro-Caribbean music, another music showcased at JazzFest, comes from South African jive and Brazilian samba, with a touch of Jamaican reggae thrown in. Instruments include drums and thumb piano.

Festival-goers are often spotted carrying poles that represent their particular group, such as the Snake Club, whose members wear the likeness of a snake on homemade buttons. Some recent JazzFest performers include Walter Payton, Tony Green, Bamboula 2000, the Antioch Gospel Singers, Irma Thomas, Al Hirt, C.J. Chenier & the Red Hot Louisiana Band, Buckwheat Zydeco, BeauSoleil, Snooks Eaglin, Bruce Hornsby, Pete Fountain, the Neville Brothers, and Mary Chapin Carpenter.

If you love jazz, food, and the swampy sounds of zydeco music, then New Orleans in late April is the place to be. JazzFest, which may just be the ultimate New Orleans cultural experience, is a living tribute to the spasm bands,

Storyville professors, and jazz musicians of the past whose gutsy spirits live on in the City That Care Forgot.

Nightspots

House of Blues, 225 Decatur St.; (504) 529-2624
Palm Court Jazz Cafe, 1204 Decatur St.; (504) 525-0300
Pat O'Brien's, 718 St. Peter; (504) 561-1200
Richelieu Room (Arnaud's), 813 Bienville; (504) 523-2847
Rhythms, 227 Bourbon St.; (504) 523-3800
Tipitina's, 501 Napoleon Ave.; (504) 895-8477

JazzFest Information—(504) 522-4786

Voodoo
—*African Spiritism, Magic Spells, and Marie Laveau*

Voodoo, the mysterious cult of spiritism, had its origins in Africa, specifically in the Republic of Benin (formerly Dahoney), where *Vodu* was a Dahomean religion that was animist in nature (worshipped animals), one of the main gods being Zombi, a giant snake. The religion has also been known as vodu, voudou, vaudau, and hoodoo; in fact, modern followers prefer the term "verdoun." It often involved drinking of blood, black magic, bizarre cult ceremonies, and violent sex orgies. Today, in Hispanic cultures, it is referred to as "Santeria."

Carried across the ocean by an enslaved people to Haiti and New Orleans, the rituals and black magic spells associated with voodoo converted many followers. After its arrival in New Orleans, voodoo also incorporated many Catholic Church beliefs in its rituals. Some of the claims, such as clawing each other bloody during frenzied ceremonies and small coffins at the rituals that contained kidnapped and sacrificed Creole babies, induced great fear of voodoo among the New Orleans population in general.

Voodoo Queen

A matriarchy, the power of voodoo allegedly belonged to the high priestess, who was always a free woman of color. Many held the office, including Sanite DeDe, a voodoo queen who was said to have held the first organized ceremony in an abandoned brickyard on Dumaine Street. She also sold sweetmeats in front of the Cabildo during the week and presided over dances in Congo Square on Sundays. Many of the ceremonies took place around bayous and lakes surrounding the city, particularly Bayou St. John.

The first recorded voodoo "doctor," Doctor John, John Montenet (from whom the singer took his name) had a house on Bayou St. John during the 1840s filled with a harem of female slaves. A heavily tattooed voodoo practitioner who claimed to be a Senegalese prince, Doctor John exerted a great deal of power over New Orleans slaves and paid local household servants to spy for him. He then sold their secrets, which he used to convince followers of his power. Doctor John was famous for astrology, mind reading, and black magic.

Marie Laveau (c. 1796-1881)

The most famous voodoo queen of all was none other than Marie Laveau. A tall woman whose Grecian profile resembled a black Athena, Marie was born of a mulatto and a wealthy white planter. Marie married Jacques Paris in 1819 at the St. Louis Cathedral in New Orleans. Paris, a native of Haiti, disappeared mysteriously shortly after the marriage, and his devout Catholic wife began calling herself the Widow Paris.

The Widow Paris worked as a hairdresser for fashionable Creole women and eventually became the mistress of Louis Christophe Duminy de Glapion. The two had fifteen children and lived in a house on St. Ann Street. What caused Marie's move into voodoo is not known, but by the time of her death in 1881, she ruled believers and nonbelievers alike, including high government officials, throughout the New Orleans community. Her unique combination of religion with black magic held the entire city in awe of her power. Black servants used to threaten their white charges that "Marie Laveau will come get you!" to terrorize them into behaving.

The tall beauty was known for her long gold earrings and the blue tignon tied around her head. She often wore a blue dress also, because the color blue represented spirituality. Her cottage on St. Ann, between Rampart and Burgundy, was reputedly given to her by a New Orleans merchant whose son was found innocent of a crime after Marie put three peppers in her mouth, went to the St. Louis Cathedral for several hours the day of the boy's trial, and then hid the peppers under the judge's chair in the Cabildo. The young man was found innocent.

Marie Laveau, high priestess of voodoo. *New Orleans Historic Voodoo Museum*

Marie began to gain her power during the 1830s, when she was feared by slaves everywhere and was also called on by Creole women who consulted with her for help in matters of the heart. It was said that she even influenced judges and politicians. Marie often invited the public, including police and city officials, to her voodoo rites along Bayou St. John. Every St. John's Eve (June 23), there was a massive exodus to the bayou to observe the sacred voodoo day, which was also sacred to John the Baptist. Saint John's Eve has been celebrated since ancient times, when European pagan sun worshipers rolled wheels of fire down hills as the sun descended.

It was said by observers that Marie sat on an elevated throne-like chair in front of a roaring bonfire directing the glistening, dancing bodies of worshipers. Secret voodoo meetings were held along nearby Lake Pontchartrain, reportedly in a small white cottage, where animal sacrifice, snake worship, blood drinking, and sex orgies took place. It was reported that young white women sometimes participated in these events.

Drinking Tafia

The followers drank tafia, a drink similar to rum, in order to intoxicate themselves during the rites. Another mixture, also called tafia, contained red wine, cinnamon, and various herbs and spices, which were all heated in a large kettle during the ceremony. The drinks incited participants to strip and begin their dancing and shrieking to the gods.

Marie also sold love charms, amulets, and gris-gris, which was a bag filled with special charms, either for good or bad luck. Gris-gris, the infamous black or red bag of "charms," contained anything from human hair, snakeskins, or dead lizards to graveyard dust. These bags, which are sold today in New Orleans, are used to cross an enemy or to ward off bad luck. They are usually tied with seven knots. One unusually powerful gris-gris bag was supposedly made from the shroud of a dead person and contained a dried one-eyed toad, a dried lizard, the little finger of a black person who had committed suicide, the wings of a bat, the eyes of a cat, the heart of a rooster, and the liver of an owl. Other popular "curses" were sprinkling powders on the steps of an enemy's house, leaving a dead chicken at their doorstep, or forming a cross of salt in front of their dwelling.

To Make a Love Powder

Gut a live hummingbird. Dry the heart and powder it. Sprinkle the powder on the person you desire.

Marie also was an astute businesswoman, who, as a black woman, used the cult to earn not only fame but also wealth. Stories abound of her cunning activities, such as using knowledge of an extramarital affair to blackmail New Orleans gentlemen, then offering "cures" to the unsuspecting wife (whom Marie informed) for her husband's infidelity. The cunning priestess was usually rewarded by both husband and wife for her "favors."

For favorable court decisions, Laveau would write the names of jury members, the judge, and the prosecuting attorney on a piece of paper, then place the paper into a chipped hole in a block of ice that was covered with powdered sugar. At that point, Laveau and her client would lie on their backs on the floor near the ice, rap nine times on the floor, and recite prayers.

Voodoo and Catholicism

In her later years the voodoo queen became known for her visits to condemned prisoners, who would watch with sadness as the unofficial "spiritual adviser" prepared an altar consisting of a box about three feet square with three pyramid-shaped boxes on top, and a small figure of the Virgin Mary placed on the apex. Laveau also brought the prisoners bowls of gumbo and platters of fried fish. Marie, who always

37

claimed to be a devout Catholic, was said to have gone to mass almost daily during her life.

Another story of Laveau's cunning and charity tells of the time a destitute, ragged young man came to her door begging for money. She had the man lie on a couch in her front room, covered him with a sheet, and placed lighted candles at his head and feet. The priestess then sat on her front doorstep, tin cup in hand, begging for money to pay for the poor man's funeral. It was not long before she had sufficient funds to take care of both herself and the newly recovered "corpse."

Gris-Gris for a Successful Marriage

Join the hands of two dolls with a ribbon. Take some sand and pile it up in a mound. On top of this place nine wax candles, sprinkle the whole with champagne saying, "St. Joseph, make this marriage, and I'll pay." When the marriage takes place, put a plate of macaroni sprinkled with parsley near a tree in Congo Square for payment.

A few months before her death, Marie Laveau was visited by writer George W. Cable, who described the voodoo queen as follows.

> ...Her dwelling was in a quadroon quarter of New Orleans, but a step or two from Congo Square, a small adobe cabin just off the sidewalk....In the center of a small room whose ancient cypress floor was worn with scrubbing and sprinkled with crumbs of soft brick—a Creole affectation of superior cleanliness—sat quaking with feebleness in an ill-looking old rocking-chair, her body bowed, and her wild, gray witch's tresses hanging about her

shriveled yellow neck, the Queen of the Voodoos. . . .
They said she was over one hundred years old, and
there was nothing to cast doubt upon the statement.
She had shrunken away from her skin; it was like a
turtle's. Yet withal one could hardly help but see
that the face, now so withered, had once been
handsome and commanding. There was still a faint
shadow of departed beauty on the forehead, the
spark of an old fire in the sunken, glistening eyes,
and a vestige of imperiousness in the fine, slightly
aquiline nose, and even about her silent woebegone
mouth.

There is a great deal of controversy regarding Marie Laveau's
daughter, Marie Laveau II, born in 1827. Some writers say she
never existed and was only a phantom who appeared after
the first Marie died. Others say the daughter was exiled by
the family after her mother's death, and still other sources
report that Marie II was actually more popular than Marie I.
There was a daughter named Marie born to Laveau in 1827,
but it is not known whether Parish or Glapion was the girl's
father. A Marie Philome Glapion who died in 1897 is listed on
the old marker of the Laveau tomb in St. Louis No. 1
Cemetery.

Sources do seem to agree that a Malvina Latour became the
voodoo queen of New Orleans after Marie Laveau's death,
with Marie's blessing, and it is possible she was mistaken for
Marie's daughter, because she practiced for many years while
Marie was alive (Laveau more or less "retired" from the ceremonies after 1869). Marie Laveau II was believed to have
started the Friday visits to the infamous Wishing Stump along
Bayou St. John.

When Marie died in 1881, she was described as a "good
mother, a good friend and regretted by all who knew her,"

Marie Laveau, shortly before her death. Magazine reproduction, 1886. *Historic New Orleans Collection*

although others believed she was the "devil incarnate" and were relieved that she was gone. Voodoo is practiced today in New Orleans, but it is a much tamer version of the old voodoo. Shops in the French Quarter sell dolls, black candles, and gris-gris bags.

The New Orleans Historic Voodoo Museum, located at 724 Dumaine Street, has a collection of photographs, gris-gris potions, a live python, altars, masks, and even a spiritual adviser and a voodoo priestess. The group also conducts walking, swamp, and plantation tours.

———————————

New Orleans Historic Voodoo Museum
724 Rue Dumaine; (504) 523-7685
Adults $6.30

Literary New Orleans

The great Mississippi, the ancient courtyards, shadowy alleys, and rich fumes of river water and spicy cooking combine to give New Orleans a flavor like no other city. Samuel Clemens first used "Mark Twain" (taken from a riverboat expression) as his pen name in an article he wrote for the *Crescent* newspaper.

Early New Orleans literature was written in French and influenced by French romanticism. Two early poets were Dominique and Adrien Roquette, brothers who came to New Orleans from France. Adrien became a priest and missionary to the Choctaw Indians and wrote *La Nouvelle Atala* based on his experiences.

The first publication of poetry by people of color in America was produced in New Orleans in 1845 and was titled *Les Cenelles*. It contained eighty-five poems written by seventeen authors. Another well-known author during the nineteenth century was novelist Dr. Alfred Mercier. One of Mark Twain's contemporaries was George Washington Cable, a New Orleans writer who gained a national reputation with his stories and novels about the Creoles.

Kate Chopin, a renowned author of short stories and novels, lived in New Orleans for a while, and part of her most famous work, *The Awakening*, is based in New Orleans. It was published in 1899 and caused a great scandal with its theme of extramarital affairs.

Many authors, such as Lyle Saxon, Lillian Hellman, Harnett T. Kane, O. Henry (William S. Porter), Francis Parkinson Keyes, and Truman Capote either called New Orleans home or were frequent visitors to the city. Thick, humid New Orleans air seemed to foster inspiration. Always bohemian, New Orleans in the 1920s was America's version of Paris' Left Bank. The early works of such literary notables as William Faulkner, Sherwood Anderson, and Ernest Hemingway were featured in the *Double Dealer*, a literary magazine of this period.

Thomas Lanier "Tennessee" Williams first came to New Orleans in 1938 and fell in love with the city. The young writer was hoping to gain employment in the city's Federal Writers' Project, under the guidance of Lyle Saxon.

The French Quarter at that time was a very laid back, more or less slum area with a distinctive Latin flavor. Living quarters were cheap, and life was easy and casual. It was not until after World War II that the French Quarter experienced a great tourist boom.

The great playwright described life in the Quarter best in his masterpiece, *A Streetcar Named Desire*, in which there are raucous fights, card games, and lovemaking to all hours. The entire play is full of the languid sensuality of the old French Quarter. *Streetcar* brought unprecedented fame to New Orleans and respect for its significance as a city in the new South. Every March, New Orleans hosts the Tennessee Williams/New Orleans Literary Festival, featuring literary tours, plays, and readings.

John Kennedy Toole's Pulitzer Prize-winning novel, *A Confederacy of Dunces*, brought more fame to New Orleans, particularly to Lucky Hot Dog vendors. The book is about Ignatius Reilly, a Lucky vendor who makes his living in the French Quarter. Unfortunately, Toole committed suicide in 1969 at the age of thirty, before his novel was published. After a great deal of effort, his mother was able to get a sympathetic Lyle Saxon to recommend that Louisiana State University Press publish the book, and it went on to win the Pulitzer.

Another major American writer, Ellen Gilchrist, grew up in New Orleans and used it as a setting for many of her short stories. One of the more popular contemporary writers of New Orleans fame is Anne Rice, whose *Chronicle of the Vampires* series have spawned throngs of thrill-seeking sightseers who search for the locations of Rice's scenes, such as graveyards and Garden District mansions.

Lucky Hot Dog vendor, made famous in John Kennedy Toole's *A Confederacy of Dunces*.

Many movies, such as *The Big Easy* and *Tightrope*, have been set in New Orleans. While the French Quarter now contains more tourists than it does artists and writers, New Orleans continues to lure aspiring authors with its ageless appeal to the senses.

———

See *Kate Chopin*

Mardi Gras—*Carnival Season*

Only in the City That Care Forgot can one find the greatest free show on earth—Mardi Gras, or Carnival, as the locals refer to it. The season of delightful madness begins each year on January 6th (Twelfth Night—the twelfth day after Christmas). Mardi Gras continues through Fat Tuesday itself (*Mardi Gras* means Fat Tuesday in French).

The day following Mardi Gras is Ash Wednesday, and it marks the beginning of Lent, a time of fasting that occurs before Easter. Easter is the first Sunday after the full moon following the spring equinox, March 21. Since Mardi Gras occurs forty-six days before Easter, the actual date varies, so the holiday is usually, but not always, in February.

History of Carnival

The history of Mardi Gras celebrations in New Orleans is somewhat vague, but elaborate subscription balls were very much a part of the city's social life in the early 1800s. In 1827 a group of young men organized a street parade of maskers. The parade was such a success that it was repeated each year, and in 1837 the first floats appeared in the procession. The throwing of sweetmeats to young ladies who viewed the parades from their balconies were the first Mardi Gras "throws."

It was not until 1857, however, that the Mystic Krewe of Comus was formed. "Krewes" are clubs that organize their own parades and celebrations each year during Carnival. "Comus" is derived from the Greek word for revelers, "Komos."

The winter Carnival celebrations were actually pagan in origin, and most drew their themes from Greek mythology.

Christian leaders attempted to "legitimize" the revelry by making it coincide with the traditional Catholic religious observances of Lent and Easter. The early parades were night parades with flambeaux (torches) lighting the way.

It was not long before Carnival grew to a citywide celebration of parades and masked balls that attracted tourists from all over the country. With only a few exceptions, such as world wars, Mardi Gras continued to be held with growing popularity.

The early *bals masqués* were both public and private, most of them extracting a sum of money from attendees. The balls proved to be very successful and were usually held in theaters. For a time, the Spaniards attempted to outlaw masking, due to various scandals and murders, and forbade racial mixing at the balls. These edicts were not too effective and did not last long.

During the mid-1820s, celebrations known as "Carnival Tableau Balls" became fashionable. These balls started out with a theatrical presentation, followed by dancing and a festive supper. Public balls during this time continued to be raucous affairs, and in 1825 citizens attempted (without success) to convince city aldermen to outlaw all masked balls again. It was also during this period that the quadroon balls became well-known, and it was common for Creole gentlemen to excuse themselves from the polite society balls for the excitement offered by the quadroon ladies, leaving frustrated Creole maidens to work on their tapestry projects.

Street parades, meanwhile, were growing larger and more elaborate each year. A group of prominent citizens, the Bedouins, paraded in 1841 with over 300 paraders in bright costumes. Other maskers joined them as the Bedouins passed, and by 1832, theirs was a march of thousands.

The Twelfth Night Revelers presented the first Mardi Gras queen in 1871, and in the following year the first daytime parade was given by Rex, the King of Carnival. This procession came about due to a visit by the Russian Grand Duke Alexis Romanoff, who was in New Orleans reputedly to visit a singer, Lydia Thompson. Miss Thompson was starring in a play, *Blue Beard*, and a tune from the show, "If Ever I Cease to Love," was played during the parade. The song has been Carnival's theme song ever since. It was during this same period that Mardi Gras' official flag and colors were carried—purple for justice, gold for power, and green for faith.

The first all-female Mardi Gras parade was in 1941, presented by the Krewe of Venus, although Mardi Gras' first female krewe organized a ball back in 1896. The famous Zulu Krewe (Zulu Aid and Pleasure Club), Carnival's first African-American krewe, began parading in 1909. Louis Armstrong was the Zulu King in 1949. Zulus are famous for tossing hand-painted coconuts to the crowds.

In his book *Fabulous New Orleans*, writer Lyle Saxon describes a childhood Mardi Gras around the turn of the century:

> . . . The maskers on the floats were throwing trinkets to the crowd in the street—beads, tiny bags of sweetmeats, metal ornaments. And upon coming close to one car, I saw that each masker was provided with a silken bag which matched his costume—and it was from these bags that the bagatelles were produced and flung toward the outstretched hands below.
>
> At last the parade left Canal Street and entered Bourbon Street, a narrow thoroughfare which led toward the French Opera House. So narrow was the street that the great decorated cars covered it from sidewalk to sidewalk, and the maskers who rode

high on top of the cars were almost level with the
balconies of wrought iron which overhung the street
.... It was here that I realized the hugeness of these
moving cars—for, filling the street as they did, and
lumbering over the rough pavement, the great
glittering masses seemed as incredible as though the
very houses were gliding past.

The Celebration Today

Today's Carnival is best known for exotic and bizarre costumes, elaborate floats, and cries of, "Throw me something,
Mister!" from the throngs of people packing the streets. Popular throws include beads, doubloons (aluminum coins
emblazoned with the krewe's emblem), plastic cups, and trin-
kets of all sorts. These dubious treasures are highly prized,
and people will fight and knock each other over in a mad
scramble for the souvenirs. Savvy Carnival-goers know to put
their foot on the item to facilitate eventual retrieval.

Carnival season, as previously mentioned, begins January 6,
usually with private balls. These balls continue until the last
two weeks before Mardi Gras, when the partying and parading get serious. Every day during the final two weeks, parades
march through the streets. The krewes, which sponsor the
parades, are headed by captains, whose identities often
remain secret. There are approximately sixty krewes that
sponsor parades, and most also have kings and queens.

The most famous krewe is that of Rex, King of Mardi Gras,
whose arrival is the highlight of Carnival festivities. Rex and
his parade arrive on the actual date of Mardi Gras. Celebrities
traditionally serve as the King of Carnival, and past kings
include Drew Carey, John Goodman, Henry Winkler, and
Harry Connick Jr. When Rex and his court meet the Mystic

Krewe of Comus later that night, it marks the closing event of Carnival.

People often wonder how Mardi Gras is organized, and the answer is that it really isn't, except by the independent krewes. Each krewe is autonomous and, although it observes the traditional parade dates, sponsors and pays for its own balls and parades. When you think about it, it's pretty remarkable that so many huge parties and parades are carried off.

> *It is a custom to which the citizens were and their descendants are much attached, and it will be difficult to prevent its continuance.*
>
> American visitor
> observing Mardi Gras in 1835

The King Cake Tradition

Any New Orleans celebration would be incomplete without food, and Mardi Gras is no exception. The sweet bakery concoction known as a "king cake" resembles a large coffee cake, and it is decorated with sprinkles of yellow, green, and purple. King cakes are baked with either a bean or a tiny plastic baby (supposed to be the Baby Jesus) inside. When the cake is served at Mardi Gras parties, whoever receives the slice with the object traditionally sponsors the next party or buys the next king cake.

Local bakeries ship thousands of king cakes across the country each year to would-be Mardi Gras-goers. Along with the king cake, the packages usually contain Mardi Gras beads, a mask, and doubloons. So whether you live in San Francisco or New York, you can still get a piece of Mardi Gras delivered to your doorstep in honor of the festivities.

Mardi Gras Indians

One of the more interesting and colorful groups of Carnival revelers are the Mardi Gras Indians, whose sequined and feathered costumes and headdresses are sometimes the most dazzling to be found in the city. The tribes originated in the late 1800s, possibly as a tribute to the regal image of Native Americans. The custom of dressing and parading as Indians was adapted by some members of New Orleans' black community, who combined the spectacular tribal dress with the rhythm of African drumming and dancing.

It is thought that the history of Mardi Gras Indians goes all the way back to the 1790s, when Chickasaws hid escaped slaves. Since that time, the blacks honored Native Americans in their oral histories and later in the pleasure clubs. Eventually, groups dressed in feathers and headdresses and began dancing in the streets during Carnival festivities.

The first recorded Mardi Gras Indian tribe was the Creole Wild West Tribe, formed by Becate Battiste in the 1880s. Various other tribes soon sprang up, and there were often rivalries and fighting between them. Mardi Gras was traditionally considered a day to settle grudges, and the masked reveling provided a perfect opportunity for gang warfare. Today the celebrations among the tribes are generally peaceful.

A chief leads each tribe, and most tribal members come from the same inner-city neighborhoods. A few of today's tribes are the Yellow Pocahontas, Wild Tchoupitoulas, Wild Apaches, and the Ninth Ward Hunters. The Wild Tchoupitoulas recorded an album of traditional tribal songs with the Neville Brothers.

> *Always, there are two parts to Endymion, the prince of Mardi Gras parades. The first is getting there, a logistical feat that requires luck, planning and, preferably, friends nearby. But when dusk arrives and the giant convoy rolls, there are few Carnival spectacles to match the cheering crowds, the flashing lights and the storm of trinkets that rains down for hours on end.*
>
> The Times-Picayune, 2/22/98

The marching ranks usually begin with the First Spy Boy, followed by the First Flag Boy, other tribal members, the carrier of the Gang Flag, the Medicine Man, the Second Chief, and finally the Big Chief himself. The marchers are accompanied by much shouting and chanting. A single costume with its elaborate plumage can cost thousands of dollars. The energy and colorful showmanship of the Mardi Gras Indians are one of the most exciting spectacles of Carnival.

Secrets of Mardi Gras Regulars

Those who make Carnival an annual tradition know a few things about parade watching and participation that may not be obvious to newcomers. You may think watching a parade go by is a simple, uncomplicated, leisurely activity, but Mardi Gras regulars know better. The die-hards have specially constructed ladders that have seats attached to them so children can sit up high and watch the festivities. An ice chest with some food and plenty of their favorite beverages always accompany these fans. Lawn chairs are necessary for easily fatigued parade-watchers.

If you are planning to attend your first Mardi Gras, bring plenty of high spirit, lots of refreshments, and sunscreen. Be prepared to be shocked at the outrageous costumes, occasional nudity, and general debauchery. Just remember that at midnight, when the season of Lent begins, the streets are cleared of tons of trash, everyone goes home, and the next day, which is Ash Wednesday, it will be time to go to church and start repenting.

Mardi Gras for Families

If you find Mardi Gras a bit overwhelming, especially for family viewing, you will be happy to know about services offered to help children celebrate Mardi Gras in a safe, much tamer way. Accents on Arrangement, Inc., offers a large variety of personalized Mardi Gras tours for children. Owned by mother and former schoolteacher Diane Lyons, the service sponsors, among other things, trips to Blaine Kern's Mardi Gras World, where children can see float figures up close, mask decorating contests in the French Market, and streetcar rides on the world's oldest continuously running streetcar.

Lyons and her staff, all CPR trained and bonded, will be happy to take your child on a fun-filled Mardi Gras adventure while you enjoy the adult Mardi Gras. Kids can experience cooking a king cake and learn the significance of stuffing a tiny plastic baby in the dough or take a horse-drawn buggy ride, stopping at the U.S. Mint, where Mardi Gras memorabilia is displayed, and the Musee Conti Wax Museum, where they will see a spectacular display of Mardi Gras Indians. Quality child care and entertainment is Ms. Lyons' guarantee.

In addition to Accents on Arrangement, the Louisiana Children's Museum (see *Museums*) offers Mardi Gras mask making, crafts, and second-line parading. All activities are free after admission to the museum ($5).

The Canal Street Sheraton offers Kidz Karnival Club, a package of nightly entertainment with different themes, for three-year-olds and up. The Hotel Inter Continental has a good deal—private parade reviewing stands on St. Charles Avenue. So if you're in town for Mardi Gras and want to be sure your kids have a good time, give one of these groups a call!

———

Accents on Arrangement, Inc. (504) 866-3736

Social Aid and Pleasure Clubs

During the 1880s African Americans began forming benevolent societies whose purpose was to care for social needs, including providing health care, funerals, and burials. These societies became known as "Social Aid and Pleasure Clubs," and they continue to operate to this day.

The best-known tradition of the "SA & PCs," as they are called, is their colorful brass band street parades. The parades would begin as solemn processions following a coffin to the graveyard and playing hymns and spiritual songs, such as "Flee as a Bird." After the graveyard ceremony, the paraders struck up joyful, jazzy music, as the loved one's soul entered heaven. These jazz funeral parades were very popular, and the bands soon expanded their parading to include almost any—or even no—occasion.

The tradition of street parades and second lining is seeing a rejuvenation today in New Orleans. "Second lining" means following the club members who are paralleled by the band. Each parade can cost over $5,000 by the time permits are paid, police protection is obtained, and members are outfitted

Olympia Jazz Band on Chartres Street. View of band members in the 1200 block of Chartres in the Vieux Carré conducting a mock jazz funeral. They are followed by "second-liners." *Historic New Orleans Collection*

with matching costumes. One group, the Nkruman Better Boys, wear lime-green suits, burgundy hats, and crocodile shoes. Some of the costumes cost as much as $1,200 each. The club also provides refreshments for the strutting, dancing participants.

The oldest SA & PC still in existence is the Young Men Olympian Junior Benevolent Society, formed in 1884. Jazz greats Louis Armstrong and King Oliver played with the street bands in their early days. In 1954 Armstrong wrote:

> To watch those clubs parade was an irresistible and absolutely unique experience. All the members wore full dress uniforms, and with those beautiful silk ribbons streaming from their shoulders they were a sight to see.

The parades experienced a decline during the sixties, seventies, and eighties but are now making a comeback. Members raise money throughout the year to stage their parades, which brighten and enliven New Orleans streets on Sundays from August through May. Even women now have marching clubs, such as the Original New Orleans Lady Backjumpers. The people of New Orleans don't need a reason to play music, dance, and have a good time!

Algiers—The Forgotten New Orleans

A pleasant ferry ride across the Mississippi will take you to the community on the West Bank known as Algiers. There is actually a twenty-seven-mile strip of communities along the West Bank—Algiers, Gretna, Harvey, Marrero, and Westwego —but only Algiers is incorporated as part of New Orleans and is the fifteenth ward of the city. Although some New Orleans citizens refuse to acknowledge Algiers as part of the city, Algiers has a rich and proud heritage. When Bienville laid out New Orleans in 1718 he set aside a tract of land on the West Bank of the river. (Some say he chose the best for himself.) Developer John Law established the Company Plantation (later the King's Plantation) in the same area, and these two holdings became present-day Algiers.

There has been a great deal of speculation about the origin of Algiers' name, but the most likely story is that one of Governor Alexander O'Reilly's soldiers who had participated in a campaign against Algeria gave it the name. Much of the West Bank was eventually settled by plantation owners who built mansions on their estates. The Mississippi played a major role in the development of Algiers. Before the levee was built, severe floods wiped out homes, farms, and businesses during the years 1865, 1884, 1895, 1922, and 1927. The river also made possible the community's growth as a port, shipyard, and later a railway.

In 1805 Barthélemy Duverjé acquired much of the land that makes up the present community and built a plantation home there in 1812. The home was later destroyed by fire. The West Bank figured prominently in the Battle of New Orleans during the months of December 1814 and January 1815, when General Andrew Jackson's forces defeated the British.

The actual battles were mostly fought in Chalmette, which is downriver from Algiers.

Two historic figures from Algiers are particularly noteworthy. One is John McDonogh (1779-1850), a philanthropist who left a fortune for public education. He lived in the plantation home of Monplasir, which was destroyed during a levee breakage in 1861. At his death, the New Orleans businessman left an estate valued at over two million dollars.

Sketch of a typical plantation house.

Martin Behrman, another citizen of the Algiers community, served as mayor of New Orleans for seventeen years, the longest of any mayor up to this point. He died in office in 1926. Behrman was born in New York in 1864 and moved with his family to New Orleans as an infant. After his marriage to Julia Collins, he settled in Algiers and entered the mercantile business.

Algiers was known also for its shipbuilding yards, port, and railway. By 1881 Algiers had twenty dry docks and had built a number of Civil War battleships. With New Orleans growing as a port city, industry in Algiers continued to grow as well. The railroad moved in, and Algiers eventually became the eastern terminus of Southern Pacific's Louisiana to California run.

One of the oldest landmarks in Algiers is the naval station, which was officially opened in 1901 and played a prominent role during the two world wars as a base for outfitting and repairing ships and also as a training center. In 1958 the new Mississippi River Bridge opened, finally connecting Algiers to downtown New Orleans. After the bridge opened, Algiers experienced dramatic growth.

Today Algiers is a charming community with quaint historic houses that tell the story of its past. It is well worth a ferry ride (that's the best way to go) over the river to see Algiers and is definitely something the whole family will enjoy.

———

Ferry $1 per person

New Orleans Places and Family Activities

A Must-See Guide for Visitors
— *Jackson Square, Café du Monde, Cabildo, St. Charles Avenue, etc.*

The best way to see the French Quarter is on foot; in fact, some of the streets are closed to automobiles during certain hours. The following guide will take you along a route of historic streets, shops, and buildings. If you can, it's a good idea to take at least two days to tour the Quarter. History lovers could spend endless days in just the Cabildo, which housed the government under Spanish rule and today is filled with historical artifacts. So put on your walking shoes and explore!

> *Patrolman Mancuso inhaled the moldy scent of the oaks and thought, in a romantic aside, that St. Charles Avenue must be the loveliest place in the world. From time to time he passed the slowly rocking streetcars that seemed to be leisurely moving toward no special destination, following their route through the old mansions on either side of the avenue.*
>
> *A Confederacy of Dunces*
> John Kennedy Toole

The Mississippi River Levee and Jackson Square

Start your tour by walking through the heart of the French Quarter, Jackson Square, and take in the artists, old buildings, carriages, and colorful vendors. The majestic statue of Andrew Jackson on his horse dominates the square. The famous equestrian statue was commissioned by Baroness Micaela de Pontalba.

Jackson Square. *Photo by Grant L. Robertson*

Jackson Square is famous for its artists, street vendors, tarot card readers, and tourists. It is fascinating to observe the artists in action. Cross Decatur Street and you are on the levee, where you can sit on a bench and watch the ships and barges coming and going. Then wander over to Café du Monde for beignets and café-au-lait. Beignets are rectangular deep-fried doughnuts dipped in powdered sugar. They are addictive! Café-au-lait is a drink that is equal parts strong coffee (often flavored with chicory) and steamed milk.

Beignets inside Café du Monde c. 1940. *Historic New Orleans Collection*

Most of the following sites are within the French Quarter and can be easily found on a map.

They told me to take a streetcar named Desire, and then transfer to one called Cemeteries and ride six blocks and get off at —Elysian Fields!

Blanche DuBois
A Streetcar Named Desire
Tennessee Williams

The Cabildo

Flanking Jackson Square and one of New Orleans' most famous structures is the old heart of Spanish government, the Cabildo. It has been carefully preserved by the Louisiana State Museum and Friends of the Cabildo and today houses a spectacular museum of Louisiana historical artifacts and documents. It has survived several fires and was closed for six years at one point, reopening in 1994 after a $6 million restoration.

The original building was constructed beginning in 1795, with funds donated by Don Almonester y Roxas, who also donated money for St. Louis Cathedral. On the second floor, in 1803, transfer papers for the Louisiana Purchase were signed.

Among the countless historical items on view are Napoleon's death mask, an Indian pirogue (dugout boat), weapons, and artifacts from daily life in Louisiana's colorful past. History buffs will think they're in heaven in the restored Cabildo.

Pontalba Apartments

On either side of Jackson Square are the Pontalba Apartments, one of the most prestigious addresses in the Crescent City. Excellent examples of unique New Orleans architecture, the buildings are among the oldest apartment dwellings in the United States. The famous two identical residential structures were commissioned by Micaela Almonester, baroness de Pontalba (1795-1874), whose fiery temper drove her father-in-law to shoot her in the chest and then kill himself. She survived the wound and left Paris for New Orleans, where she owned property at the Place d'Armes (Jackson Square). The baroness had the apartments built and supervised much of the construction herself. (Not open to the public.)

See *Micaela de Pontalba*

St. Louis Cathedral

The oldest continually active cathedral in the United States, the St. Louis Cathedral was originally constructed in 1724 and was a wooden structure which burned in 1788. Don Andre Almonester y Roxas, the father of Micaela de Pontalba, gave money for a new cathedral to be built, which opened in 1794. Notice the beautiful stained glass windows, murals, and frescoes. The present building dates from 1851. Guided tours are available.

Presbytére

Now a part of the Louisiana State Museum complex and to the right as you face the cathedral, the Presbytére was built as a home for priests, although it was never used for that purpose. Among other things, it was once used as a courthouse. Today it contains historical exhibits.

Ursuline Convent

In August of 1727 a small group of Ursuline nuns arrived in New Orleans from France. Their mission was to establish a girls' school and care for the sick. Shortly after the arrival of the nuns came the so-called "casket girls" (see Famous and Infamous People). The Sisters occupied a building at 301 Chartres Street until the present structure was completed in 1753. Located at 1114 Chartres, the Ursuline Convent was one of the only buildings in the city to survive the devastating fire of March 21, 1788, and many local historians believe the convent is the Quarter's oldest building. Certainly the ancient structure is a rare example of pure French Creole architecture, with its dormer windows and portico.

The convent was designed in 1745 by Ignance François Broutin, a Louisiana engineer. Now housing St. Mary's Church, the convent remains rich with history. Walk through the guarded gates, peaceful corridors, and arched doorways, and imagine the thousands of girls and nuns who walked the same paths to their studies and prayers. The convent was home to the country's first nunnery, all girls' school, Indian school, and Negro school.

––––––

1114 Chartres Street
Limited public tours

Cornstalk Fence and Hotel

This French Quarter landmark is known for the ripened ears of corn made of cast ironwork that decorate the fence in front of the Victorian structure. The story behind the famous ears of corn is that they were commissioned by a doctor who owned the house during the 1800s. It seems his wife, a Midwesterner, was homesick for her native land and the endless fields of corn.

Today the home has been converted to The Cornstalk Fence Hotel and is elegantly furnished with antique beds and crystal chandeliers. Located at 915 Royal Street in the heart of the French Quarter, the hotel was also home in the early 1800s to Judge Francis-Xavier Martin, first Chief Justice of the Louisiana Supreme Court and author of the first history of Louisiana. Harriet Beecher Stowe was also a guest here and was inspired to write *Uncle Tom's Cabin* after viewing nearby slave auction markets.

Cornstalk Fence Hotel with ironwork corn stalks.

Lalaurie House

At 1140 Royal Street (corner of Governor Nicholls) stands a very old structure known as The Haunted House. Its history is sordid enough to make a casual observer cross to the other side of the street and hurry past the house whose activities shocked even the most jaded of New Orleans citizens.

Writer George W. Cable visited the haunted house in the late 1880s when he was researching his book *Strange True Stories of Louisiana*. At the time of his visit, the stucco-covered brick house rose four stories high, its unusual garrets, sloping roof, barricaded doors, and battened shutters mute testimony to the horrors that took place inside the house. It is not known

65

when the house was built exactly; some say the late 1700s, but houses were not built so tall at that time. It is known, however, that in 1831 the property was sold to a Madame Marie Delphine McCarty Lalaurie, a beautiful Creole woman who had had several husbands. Her current husband, who was younger than she, was Dr. Louis Lalaurie. Ironically, the property was located only a block away from the Ursuline Convent.

The Lalauries were wealthy Creoles who entertained lavishly in their elegantly furnished mansion on Royal Street. Madame Lalaurie was seen riding about New Orleans every evening in her coach, driven by a black servant. She also had two daughters by her previous marriages. As the elegant Creole lady and her husband rose in the swirl of New Orleans society, rumors began to circulate that the household slaves (there were nine besides the coachman) were being mistreated by Madame Lalaurie and that they were hollow-chested and starving. Others said the vicious gossip was being spread by "jealous Americans."

There was during this period an intense rivalry between the Creoles and the Americans, who were beginning to exercise their governmental authority over the town. A law student was sent by an American lawyer to point out the section of the infamous *Black Code* that slaves should be properly fed, clothed, and cared for by their masters, or the master would be subject to prosecution. Apparently the messenger was so impressed by the gentility and sweet nature of Madame Lalaurie that he left thinking her completely incapable of even the slightest unkindness toward another human being.

One morning a neighbor of the house on Royal Street witnessed a black girl approximately eight years of age screaming and running in terror from Madame Lalaurie, who was chasing the child with a cowhide whip in her hand.

Apparently the child ran into the house and ascended stairway after stairway, finally running shrieking onto the roof of the house. According to the neighbor's account, the little girl scrambled about the roof, until there was the sound of a thud on the paved court far below, and the child's lifeless body was taken up and out of sight.

This matter was reported to the authorities, and there are varying accounts of what, if any, punishment was meted out to Madame Lalaurie. Some say she was merely fined for cruelty to her slaves; other accounts reported that her slaves were taken from her and sold to her relatives, who in turn sold them back to the Madame. There was not a body to prove anything; only the account of the neighbor.

Everything came to light April 10, 1834, when an aging house servant, who was chained to the wall, purposely set the house on fire. As neighbors and passersby rushed to save those inside the smoldering mansion, Madame Lalaurie kept insisting that her porcelain, jewels, and fine furniture be brought out. When asked about the nine slaves she held, the woman was evasive, saying to never mind them now, but please save the valuables. Insistent men broke through barricaded doors in the attic of the house and what they brought below made the crowd "literally groan with horror and shouts of indignation."

The next day, the editor of the *Advertiser* described the scene as follows:

> We saw one of these miserable beings. The sight
> was so horrible that we could scarce look upon it.
> The most savage heart could not have witnessed the
> spectacle unmoved. He had a large hole in his head;
> his body from head to foot was covered with scars
> and filled with worms! The sight inspired us with so
> much horror that even at the moment of writing

this article we shudder from its effects. Those who
have seen the others represent them to be in a
similar condition.

Seven human beings were brought from the house of torture
and horror, shackled with neck and leg irons and gaunt and
wild-eyed with hunger and fear. Some had been chained so
long that they remained crippled for life. Several men had the
thought to look for buried bodies, and after some digging, an
adult's body was discovered, along with that of the dead
child. The furious crowd attempted to feed and help the
wretched prisoners, and they were carefully carried away to,
according to some reports, a prison, where they were housed
and treated. Two of the seven died within the same day.

A curious silence fell over the scene that afternoon, as people
waited for authorities to take action against Madame Lalaurie
and her husband. Apparently, she, along with her two daughters and her coachman, had barricaded themselves inside the
mansion, which remained intact. Doctor Lalaurie remained
mysteriously absent throughout the goings-on. Sometime in
the afternoon, when no action had been taken against the
Lalauries, the crowd began to grow once again, demanding
justice for the horribly inhumane treatment of the slaves.

Crowds of people began filling Royal Street as dusk
approached, and they were stunned to see Madame Lalaurie's
carriage, driven by her coachman, pull up to the entrance at
its usual hour. Almost before the people realized what was
happening, Madame Lalaurie had stepped across the sidewalk
in the midst of the throng of people and entered her carriage,
which sped away. All was not finished, however.

Attempts were made to seize the horses, turn the coach over,
and drag out its occupant, but the escape was on. As her
coachman sped away toward the old Bayou St. John Road,
attempts were made to follow Madame Lalaurie, but the evil

woman had outsmarted her pursuers. A schooner was waiting at the bayou's edge, and the Creole woman was spirited away into the bayou and the night. Her coachman returned, and before he got to Royal Street, the crowd met him, killed the horses, and broke the carriage to bits. It is not known what happened to the coachman.

The people then returned to the house on Royal Street about eight o'clock that evening. The two daughters had recently escaped by another route, but the mansion was "hermetically sealed," according to one account. "A human tempest fell upon it," writes Cable; doors and windows were broken, and people "of all classes and colors" began to ransack the place. Within one hour, a newspaper, *The Courier*, reported the next day, everything movable vanished or was smashed to bits. Stairs were pulled apart piece by piece, china was broken, bedding and table linens were thrown into the street, and furniture was taken "with pains to the third-story windows, hurled out and broken—smashed into a thousand pieces— upon the ground below." The rampage continued until the sheriff showed up and stopped the mayhem.

Notarial records show that Madame Lalaurie was in Mandeville, a nearby town, ten days later, where she executed a power of attorney to her New Orleans business agent. She was also assisted by her husband. It was said that she later went to Mobile, Alabama, where she was recognized and forced to return to her native France. Most accounts say the evil Madame Lalaurie died there; others report that her body was secretly returned to New Orleans and buried in St. Louis No. 2.

The house was sold several times and served for a while as a school for white and nonwhite students, until it was shut down. Today it is privately owned and not open to the public, but it is included on some of the "Haunted" tours given in

New Orleans. Those familiar with the house on the quiet corner of Royal and Governor Nicholls say that around dusk, shrieks of chained slaves may be heard coming from the attic of the old mansion, and if the light is right, a small form may be seen darting about on the roof, crying for her life. Mostly, they say, there exists an eternal spell of silent agony enveloping the decaying house.

1140 Royal Street
Haunted History Tours
(504) 897-2030

Gallier House

Built in 1857 by renowned architect James Gallier Jr. (1827-1868), the Gallier House at 1118-1132 Royal Street is a prime example of old New Orleans design. James Gallier Sr., an Irishman, was also an architect, and he came to New Orleans in 1834 from New York City when his son was approximately seven years old.

The senior Gallier heard of opportunities in the South, and, along with his partner Charles Dakin, began designing homes, churches, and businesses. The duo designed and built the 350-room St. Charles Hotel in 1836-37. It burned in 1851. Gallier also designed the Pontalba buildings on Jackson Square but was eventually fired from the work, although his essential design remained intact.

James Gallier Jr. was educated in New York, where he had remained with his mother due to her poor health. The son eventually moved to New Orleans and took over his father's practice, where the younger Gallier became known for his use of Italianate style, including arched windows and extensive use of cast iron.

Gallier married Josephine Villavaso (1834-1906) in 1853, and they had four daughters. The architect began building his residence at Royal Street, using brick sheathed with stucco for construction. Supported by cast-iron columns, the two-story home features a cast-iron gallery, a courtyard, and a carriage-way. Almost every room in the home has black marble mantles and extensive woodwork. The tasteful Victorian home is open to the public.

———

(504) 525-5661
Monday-Saturday, 10:00 A.M.-4:00 P.M.

* * *

See *Micaela de Pontalba*

Historic New Orleans Collection Museum/Research Center

Originally founded by General and Mrs. L. Kemper Williams, the well-endowed Historic New Orleans Collection is a dream come true for history lovers and serious researchers. The gallery is located at 533 Royal Street and features changing exhibits of New Orleans life, focusing on culture and history and showcasing rare exhibits from holdings of the Collection. There is also a shop on the premises that includes rare New Orleans books and unusual gifts. The Center's buildings are likewise historic themselves, the oldest (on Royal Street) having been built in the late eighteenth century and a survivor of the fire of 1794.

The Williams Research Center, located just around the corner at 410 Chartres Street, provides state-of-the-art access to rare books, manuscripts, drawings, maps, photographs, and arti-facts. Thousands of items are added to the collection each year by donation or purchase. The gracious and helpful staff at the Williams Research Center will assist you in finding your great-great-great-grandmother's house, a map of the city's oldest cemeteries, firsthand accounts of yellow fever epidemics, or even guide you through research on a book about the Crescent City! The Historic New Orleans Collection and its staff are well respected in the historical community for their extensive knowledge of New Orleans culture and history.

The Historic New Orleans Collection
533 Royal St.; (504) 523-4662
10:00 A.M.-4:45 P.M., Tuesday-Saturday
Admission free

The Williams Research Center
410 Chartres St.
10:00 A.M.-4:30 P.M., Tuesday-Saturday (except holidays)
Admission free

Pitot House

Located across town on serene Bayou St. John, this amazing structure was built in the 1790s and stands today as the city s oldest colonial home and an excellent example of French colonial and West Indies architectures. The home is of brick-between-post construction and was originally built by a man named Bosque. All the wood in the house is cypress, which resists rot and termites and is taken from the cypress trees that grow in the swamps. Some ten years before the French Quarter was settled (1708), houses began to be built along Bayou St. John, which had been used for years as an Indian portage. (The bayou flows into Lake Pontchartrain.)

James Francis Pitot (pronounced *Pea-tot*) was a Frenchman born Jacques François Pitot (pronounced *Pea-toe*), who moved to Haiti and left a few years later due to slave uprisings. He next moved to Philadelphia, where Pitot became an American citizen and Americanized his name, including the pronunciation of his last name.

Pitot married and moved to Spanish-ruled Louisiana in 1794 with a new bride, Jeanne Marie Carty. He was the first mayor of the incorporated city of New Orleans (serving from 1804-1805), owned a navigation company, and later served as a judge. Pitot purchased the raised plantation-style home, which later bore his name in 1810, as a country home for his family.

The stucco-covered house with its hurricane shutters, brick floors, and authentic restoration provides a fascinating look at early New Orleans life. The entire structure is designed to get maximum air circulation, and the outside galleries were built to be lived in as much as was the home's interior. There are no halls or closets, and stairways are outdoors. Most of the rooms are upstairs, where there is also a shuttered cypress sleeping porch that could be opened to feel breezes on a hot summer night. In the bedrooms, all the beds are pulled away from the wall for coolness. As in most large Southern homes, the kitchen was detached from the main house because of fire danger and heat.

The first Mrs. Pitot died in an upstairs bedroom after giving birth to twins. The twins also did not survive. Pitot remarried approximately one year later and had other children.

———

1440 Moss St. 70119
(504) 482-0312
Open Wednesday-Saturday, 10:00 A.M.-3:00 P.M.
$5 adults, $2 children

> *Everything attracts me here.*
>
> French painter Edgar Degas visiting
> relatives in New Orleans in 1872

St. Charles Avenue Streetcar Line

One of the oldest railway lines in the world in continuous operation, the St. Charles Avenue Streetcar Line, while part of the city transit system, also offers a close-up view of New Orleans' beautiful and historic Garden District. The line was originally built by the New Orleans and Carrollton Railway Company and began operation in 1835. Horse power and steam were used until 1893, when the overhead wire system now in use was installed. The cars used today, which are listed on the National Register, date from 1923-24.

The streetcars travel past such famous places as the Robert E. Lee monument (originally called Place de Tivoli), Lafayette Square, Bultman Funeral Home (where anybody who is anybody in New Orleans goes for care), Van Benthuysen House (1868-69), Christ Church Cathedral (1886), Marigny House (1856-57), and Palmer House (built in 1941 to resemble Tara in *Gone With the Wind*). Other famous places, aside from the numerous historic homes, include the Academy of the Sacred Heart (Catholic girls' school, 1900), Touro Synagogue (1909), the Mississippi River levee, shotgun houses (all rooms in a straight line with no halls), Loyola University, Tulane University, and Audubon Park.

The streetcar may be boarded at the corner of St. Charles Avenue and Common (stop #1). A round trip takes from one and one-half to two hours. The line ends at S. Claiborne Avenue and returns to Canal Street. An excellent booklet, *St. Charles Avenue Streetcar Line, A Self-Guided Tour*, is available in most gift shops for $4.95. A publication of the Historic New

Streetcars were first introduced to America in New Orleans at the 1884 Worlds Fair. The last "conventional" streetcars in regular service in the US operate today on St. Charles Avenue. *Photo by Grant L. Robertson*

Orleans Collection, this guidebook points out the famous sites and beautiful old homes along the avenue. The St. Charles Streetcar ride is a dream for lovers of history and New Orleans architecture!

One-way fare $1; return trip $1; transfer ten cents

> All of the dwellings... have a comfortable look. Those in the wealthy quarter are spacious, painted snowy white, usually, and generally have wide verandas, or double verandas, supported by ornamental columns. These mansions stand in the center of large grounds and rise, garlanded with roses, out of the midst of swelling masses of shining green foliage and many-colored blossoms.
>
> Mark Twain, visiting the Garden District

O Flaherty's Irish Channel Pub

If you want a unique French Quarter experience that the entire family will enjoy, stroll over to Danny O'Flaherty's Irish Channel Pub on Toulouse Street. Folk singer and songwriter Danny O'Flaherty is immensely popular in New Orleans and has carefully preserved his pub after the Irish tradition so that children can be comfortable there (although there is a section for adults only). In Ireland, he explains, entire families go out to have a good time at the local pubs and that is what he's doing right in the heart of the French Quarter.

O'Flaherty is also active in the Celtic Nations Heritage Festival held each October in New Orleans.

_____

514 Toulouse Street 70130
(504) 529-4570

Family Activities

New Orleans is a city filled with activities that are fun, enter-taining, and educational for the entire family. Parks, a zoo, an aquarium, streetcar rides, a river cruise, and even swamp tours (covered in *Area Outings*) offer something for everyone. So get ready to explore New Orleans and Louisiana with your family!

Audubon Zoo

From the alligator-filled swamps of Louisiana to the grass-lands of Africa, you will explore some of the Earth's most beautiful habitats and the creatures that dwell in them.

More than 1,500 animals are found in stunning natural set-tings at the Audubon Zoo. There are wooden walkways throughout the fifty-eight acres, as well as the Mombassa mini-train. Elephant and camel rides are given to children. Exhibits featuring natural habitats include the Louisiana Swamp Exhibit, Asian Domain, Australian Exhibit, and the African Savannah. Children will be delighted to watch the feeding of the sea lions.

One of the purposes of the zoo is to foster appreciation and, ultimately, conservation of these ecosystems. You come face to face with a rare white alligator and are transported by an African elephant as you make your way through the wonder-ful world of Audubon Zoo.

Throughout its history, the zoo has undergone numerous transformations. It is presently operated by the Audubon Institute, whose mission is "celebrating life through nature." A tiny group of animals introduced at Louisiana's 1884 World Exposition, mostly monkeys and birds, were the beginning of the Audubon Zoo. The animals stayed on the site of the exposition, which became known as Audubon Park, after John James Audubon, who painted many of his "Birds of America" and other wildlife images in Louisiana.

The area, which had previously hosted an Indian campsite, a sugar-processing plantation, and a Civil War hospital, became more of a zoo following the 1916 arrival of North American birds. School children collecting money paid for an elephant, and other private donations came in. The official name of the zoo was the Audubon Zoological Garden.

With the construction of several buildings by the Works Progress Administration during the 1930s, the zoo continued to grow. During the '50s and '60s, it fell into disrepair and was at one point proclaimed an "animal ghetto" by the national press. In the 1970s and '80s, the Audubon Zoo underwent several complete transformations. Today it is ranked among the nation's top zoos, hosting nearly one million visitors each year, including 150,000 school children and teachers. Friends of the Zoo, an organization founded in 1972, provides a great deal of support for the Audubon Institute, which includes not only the zoo, but Audubon Park and the Aquarium of the Americas. The zoo is located in Audubon Park.

6500 Magazine St.
(504) 861-2537
Monday-Friday, 9:30 A.M.-5 P.M.
Saturday-Sunday 9:30 A.M.-6 P.M.
Hours may change during summer months.
Adults $8; Children $4 (2-12)

Aquarium of the Americas

Located at the foot of Canal Street and the river, the Aquarium features four stunning exhibits: the Mississippi River, which has a bayou, alligators, and moss-draped trees; the Gulf of Mexico, where you can view sharks, tarpon, and stingrays through one of the world's largest underwater windows; the Caribbean Reef, featuring a transparent walk-through tunnel surrounded by coral reef, sharks, and angel fish; and the Amazon Rainforest, a jungle complete with humidity and massive vegetation. There are also touch tanks and hands-on exhibits for children (and adults).

The Aquarium operates under the auspices of the Audubon Institute. The state-of-the-art facility opened Labor Day 1990, breaking opening attendance records for aquariums everywhere. In its first full year of operation, the Aquarium hosted 2.3 million people. This educational and recreational resource, dedicated to celebrating and preserving nature, now houses the Entergy IMAX Theatre (the nation's first IMAX connected to an aquarium) and a changing exhibits gallery.

The Aquarium now also houses one of the largest and most diverse shark collections, including several species not found anywhere else in the states. You and your children can learn all about sharks—all the way from Australia's wobbegongs to Pacific reef sharks. The kids can even pet a baby shark!

After your experience at the Aquarium, stop by the River Café and enjoy a meal while viewing the great Mississippi River. You are guaranteed to be impressed!

———

Canal Street at the River
$10.50 Adults; $5 Children (2-12)
(504) 581-4629; 800-774-7394
Open daily 9:30 A.M.-6:00 P.M.

Riverboat Cajun Queen

Docked at the Aquarium of the Americas, this boat departs three times daily for narrated harbor cruises. Each cruise is an hour and a half long. Food, beverages, and a gift shop are available.

———

7 days/week 8:00 A.M.-8:00 P.M.
(504) 524-0814; 800-445-4109

Riverboat John James Audubon Aquarium/Zoo Cruise

Also docked at the Aquarium of the Americas, this popular one-hour cruise will take you back and forth between the Aquarium and the Zoo. Enjoy the ambiance of the Mississippi River and relax between tours.

———

7 days/week
800-233-2628

Storyland at City Park

This fairy-tale theme park, featuring twenty-six larger-than-life exhibits for climbing, sliding, or pretending, was rated as one of the ten best playgrounds by *Child* magazine. Storyland is also available for children's parties. The Park is located along Bayou St. John and City Park Avenue.

Streetcars Along Canal Street

While the St. Charles Avenue streetcar ride (see *Must-See Guide for Visitors*) is spectacular, the two-hour round trip may be long for young children. But they will definitely be enchanted and fascinated by the crimson and gold "Ladies in Red," as the cars are affectionately known.

Recently awarded $3.6 million in federal funds, the Regional Transit Authority maintains the charming cars, whose distinctive clangs bring back another era. Many locals use the streetcars for transportation, but there is almost always room for visitors. So hop aboard!

City Park—New Orleans' Family Playground

The fifth largest urban park in the nation, City Park of New Orleans was founded more than a century ago, when philanthropist John McDonogh gave a 100-acre tract of land to the city. Today City Park covers 1,500 acres and boasts approximately 14 million visitors each year, who come to savor its historic oak trees, distinctive statues and fountains, sports and recreation facilities, and historic buildings. (The park has the largest collection of mature live oaks in the world.)

Located in the mid-city along Bayou St. John, City Park is part of the Historic New Orleans Trace, an area that used to be a swampy, tree-filled forest that was home to Indians who used the bayou to transport goods. Many duels, or "affaires d'honneur," were fought on the land by Creole gentlemen. Dueling in the park was not outlawed until 1890.

City Park was also once the site of Allard Plantation and today is home to the New Orleans Museum of Art. Children's entertainment and leisure opportunities abound in the museum, outdoor sculptures, bridges, and seasonal programs.

See *Museums—New Orleans Museum of Art*

New Orleans Botanical Gardens

In the midst of one of the country's largest and most attractive parks, City Park, are the New Orleans Botanical Gardens. Two sisters, Eminia Wadsworth and Marion Wadsworth Harve, helped to fund the "Pavilion of the Two Sisters," an educational pavilion with a formal exhibition room, a horticultural library, and a gift shop. The facility was redeveloped in 1992 with the "old potting shed" turned into the Garden Study Center, designed to resemble an English country cottage.

A popular summer program is "Kids in the Garden," which allows children to experience planting hummingbird and butterfly gardens, water gardening, and garden photography. Not only do the children learn about plants—they also take home projects.

The beautiful garden sculptures, the aromatic garden, camellias, azaleas, antique roses, and herb garden make the New Orleans Botanical Gardens well worth a stop.

———

City Park

Louisiana Nature Center

One of the country's few wildlife preserves in an urban setting, the Louisiana Nature Center offers a planetarium, nature trails, hands-on exhibits for kids, and exhibits on Louisiana's unique environment.

———

Joe W. Brown Memorial Park
Read Blvd. at Nature Center Dr.
Tuesday-Friday, 9:00 A.M.-5:00 P.M.; Sat. 10:00 A.M.-5:00 P.M.
Sunday noon-5:00 P.M.
(504) 246-9381

Museums and Tours

New Orleans has the most unusual array of museums of any other city. Where else, for example, could you visit Mardi Gras World and see the largest fleet of carnival floats in the world or wander through the cosmos of the occult in the New Orleans Voodoo Museum? Museum-lovers will be pleased with the rich history on display around the city; even those who feel a little, well, phobic about museums will be certain to find one to their liking. And the Louisiana Children's Museum is so spectacular that it redefines the word "museum"! So prepare yourself to be impressed.

Mardi Gras World

Have you ever wondered where the gargantuan figures that sit atop huge floats come from and where they go when Carnival draws to a close? The answer to both questions is that they are stored in huge warehouses in Algiers (a community across the river from the French Quarter that is actually part of New Orleans) that are collectively called Mardi Gras World. It is here at 223 Newton Street that Blaine Kern not only houses the gigantic figures and sets but also designs and builds them, with a little help from his engineering team.

Many of the colossal figures are coated with papier-mâché or fiberglass, and they are chopped up, redesigned, and repainted year after year. Last year's John Wayne figure might be next year's Clark Gable. The floats are mounted on bases and pulled by Russian-imported tractors. Although there are other Mardi Gras warehouses, Mardi Gras World is the largest one and produces approximately forty of the sixty or so floats. Blaine also manufactures figures for other parades, such as Macy's Thanksgiving Day parade. Mardi Gras World must be seen to be believed and is open for daily tours and is easily accessible by riding the Algiers ferry at the end of Canal Street.

_____

233 Newton St. 70114
(504) 361-7821
See *Mardi Gras*

Hermann-Grima Historic House

Located in the French Quarter on St. Louis Street, the Hermann-Grima House was built in 1831 for merchant Samuel Hermann. It was one of the earliest Georgian houses built in the French Quarter. In 1844 Judge Felix Grima bought the house, and it was occupied by five generations of his family. The home is an example of American architecture and features period furniture, family portraits, loom-woven wool carpets, and silk damask draperies. During October through May, cooking demonstrations over the open hearth are given.

An unusual feature of the museum is the "Sacred to the Memory" tradition, which occurs from mid-October until All Saints' Day (November 1) and consists of a tribute to burial customs of the 1830s. Along with a casket placed in the parlor, there are black drapes covering the portraits and other mourning traditions on display. Legend says the Hermann-Grima House is haunted by a friendly ghost who lights fireplaces.

For those not in a morbid state of mind, Creole Christmas traditions are on display during the holidays, including a candlelit Christmas tree and authentic Creole Christmas decorations.

_____

820 St. Louis Street; 70130
(504) 525-5661

Louisiana Children's Museum

One of the country's top ten children's museums, the Louisiana Children's Museum boasts 45,000 square feet of fun-filled adventures, such as a math and physics lab, the *Times-Picayune* Theatre, Art Trek, a Kids' Café, Body Works, and Water Works, where you can build your own dam.

Recently the museum underwent a $2.8 million expansion. The first floor of the complex features "The Lab," a math and physics lab; "Body Works," a physical fitness exhibit sponsored by Children's Hospital; and the *"Times-Picayune* Theater," a 200-seat arena that hosts culturally diverse performances, along with plays, puppet shows, films, and demonstrations.

A particularly unique feature of the museum is Challenges, where children experience the adjustments necessary for physically challenged individuals to accomplish necessary daily tasks. Loss of hearing, sight, or movement are simulated by using headsets, goggles, and wheelchairs. They can even practice shooting baskets from a wheelchair.

The museum is housed in a building that dates from 1861 and features a combination of classic and contemporary architecture, all the way from old exposed beams and brick to a new atrium and skydome. Electrical exhibits put on continuous light shows as well. After dark the Louisiana Children's Museum hosts such events as bridal showers and corporate parties, as well as children's birthday parties and family activities.

Other unique features of the museum include a twenty-two-foot inflatable Earth balloon, which teaches children about geography; a seven-foot stuffed human ("Li'l Stuffee") with soft-sculptured organs so kids can unzip him and learn about the human body; and videos about science and nature.

There is a simulated television studio, where children can "star" as tv anchors; a mini-supermarket with cash registers, bakery, deli, and produce sections; and a playscape for one- to three-year-olds. Children can "captain" a tugboat and load sacks of coffee in a cargo net. Still other features include a French Quarter setting from the 1800s, a safety exhibit with a real car and motorcycle, a Cajun cottage where kids can "play Cajun," and a waterworks display that allows them to build dams.

The Louisiana Children's Museum is located four blocks from the Ernest N. Morial Convention Center, between Magazine and Tchoupitoulas Streets. It also contains a museum store, snack area, and party rooms. This fun and whimsical museum is definitely a hands-on experience that will be a delight to kids of all ages.

---

420 Julia Street 70130
(504) 523-1357
Tuesday-Saturday, 9:30 A.M.-4:30 P.M.
Sunday, 12:00-4:30 P.M.
Admission $5.00 per person

Musee Conti Historical Wax Museum

Children and adults will love the lifelike figures of Marie Laveau, Jean Lafitte, Louis Armstrong, Andrew Jackson, and many others. There is also a Haunted Dungeon for the brave hearts. This is a very popular museum in New Orleans, so be sure to check it out.

---

917 Conti Street
(504) 525-2605
Monday-Saturday, 10:00 A.M.-5:30 P.M.
Sunday 12:00-5:00 P.M.

Louisiana Historical Association Confederate Museum

The Confederate Museum, or Memorial Hall, as it is also known, is the oldest operating museum in Louisiana and houses one of the largest collections of Civil War artifacts in the United States. Originally opened in 1891 to store Civil War records and memorabilia, the museum was built by Frank T. Howard in memory of his father, Charles T. Howard.

A large iron cannon rests on the terrace in front of the building, and other artifacts and memorabilia include uniforms, guns, swords, mess kits, personal belongings of soldiers, and part of General Robert E. Lee's field silver service. Varina Howell Davis, widow of Confederate President Jefferson Davis, donated her husband's extensive collection of memorabilia to the museum as well. Manuscripts and documents relative to the war are numerous, and some are now housed at the Howard-Tilton Memorial Library at Tulane University for research purposes.

The original Memorial Hall was designed by New Orleans architect Thomas Sully and features brown pressed brick and arched openings in a Romanesque style. The Hall was also used as a meeting place for Confederate veterans to reflect on Civil War stories. Many tourists visit the museum, but the record number of visitors was May 27-28, 1893, when 50,000 people came to pay their respects to Jefferson Davis, who had died in New Orleans.

---

929 Camp Street 70130
(504) 523-4522
Monday-Saturday
10:00 A.M.-4:00 P.M.

New Orleans Pharmacy Museum

Built in 1853 for the United States' first licensed pharmacist, Louis Joseph Dufilho Jr., this nineteenth-century apothecary shop and courtyard herb garden contains a variety of interesting professional tools, along with facts about the practice of medicine during the nineteenth century.

––––––––

514 Chartres Street
(504) 565-8027
Tuesday-Sunday, 10:00 A.M.-5:00 P.M.
Admission $2 adults; $1 seniors/students; children under 12 free.

Longue Vue House and Gardens

This classical city estate was the home of philanthropist and businessman Edgar Bloom Stern. Stern, a New Orleans cotton broker was married to Edith, daughter of Sears CEO Julius Rosenwald. Eight acres of gardens surround the Greek Revival style mansion.

The gardens were designed by Ellen Biddle Shipman, noted "Dean of American Women Landscape Architects," and were created to complement the Spanish Court, which was inspired by the famous fourteenth-century Generalife Gardens of the Alhambra in Spain. There are other gardens on the grounds as well, such as the Wild Garden, which features natural forest walks. In cooperation with the Orleans Parish School System, Longue Vue offers fourth and fifth graders a science and social studies program.

The home itself contains the original furnishings, a gift shop, and wildflower watercolors and sculptures. The interior of the mansion, also designed by Mrs. Shipman, contains French and Oriental carpets, an antique creamware pottery collection, and American and English antiques.

_____

7 Bamboo Road 70124-1964
(504) 488-5488
Daily tours and educational programs

New Orleans Museum of Art

Founded in 1910, the New Orleans Museum of Art (NOMA) has a permanent collection of more than 35,000 objects valued in excess of $200 million. The collection is especially strong in French and American art, glass, photography, and African and Japanese works. More than 25,000 schoolchildren are given free guided tours annually.

The development of Western Civilization from the pre-Christian era to the present is emphasized. NOMA also has a unique Arts of the Americas collection that surveys the cultures of North, Central, and South America. One of the more fascinating features of the permanent collection is the work of Peter Carl Fabergé, master jeweler to the last czars of Russia. The museum sponsors many traveling exhibits as well.

"Van Go" is NOMA's museum-on-wheels, an educational liaison between the Greater New Orleans area and the museum that travels to schools around the state. The museum is a marvelous place to view art and spend a long afternoon. A gift shop and courtyard café are also on the premises.

_____

Tuesday-Sunday, 10 A.M.-5 P.M.
City Park
Adults $6; Senior Citizens $5; Children $3
(504) 488-2631

Haunted History Tours

These historic and sometimes scary tours of the French Quarter promise adventure and a fantasy-filled view of New Orleans. The Haunted History Tours explore the "grim and ghastly deeds of the old French Quarter," taking you to spots where ghosts and vampires allegedly lurk. You will see where ghosts or spirits have been sighted and see French Quarter residences in which unbelievable events took place. Several tours are offered.

The *Voodoo Cemetery Tour*, an extremely popular tour, takes visitors to the old St. Louis No. 1 Cemetery, where voodoo queen Marie Laveau is supposed to be buried. You will visit her tomb, see the marks etched on it by worshipers, and learn about the mysterious religion they practice. Tour guides even give out voodoo recipes and spells.

The *Vampire Tour* is another popular tour. Enter the macabre and unreal world of the living dead as you walk through time and experience legendary New Orleans vampires, both fictional and real. Along with sights and locations associated with the vampires, you will visit a local vampire tavern. Vampire fans will love this far-out tour! The eerie Haunted History Tours give you a good view of the darker side of New Orleans.

Haunted History Tour   2:00 P.M. daily
8:00 P.M. nightly
$15 adults, $7 children (12 and under)

Voodoo/Cemetery   10:00 A.M. daily (7 days)
1:15 P.M. daily (except Sundays)
$15 adults, $7 children (12 and under)

Both tours last 2-2½ hours and depart from Zombie's Coffee Bar at 725 St. Peter. Reservations are not required; show up 15 minutes ahead of time.

Vampire Tour 8:30 P.M. nightly (7 days)
$15 adults, $7 children (12 and under)
Departs from the front steps of the St. Louis Cathedral; reservations not required.
(504) 897-2030

Five Star Garden District Walking Tour

Stroll past the most lush and serene section of New Orleans—perhaps its most beautiful, the Garden District. Also called the "American" section of town (due to the influx of Americans in the early 1800s), the Garden District will charm you with its quiet splendor. The walking tour includes the home where Jefferson Davis, President of the Confederacy, died, author Anne Rice's home, Lafayette Cemetery, and many other antebellum homes.

———

10:00 A.M.; 1:30 P.M.
$15 Adults, $7 children (12 and under)
Meets in the lobby of the Ramada Plaza,
2203 St. Charles Avenue
Reservations not required; meet 15 minutes before departure.
(504) 897-2030

Area Outings for Families
Exploring South Louisiana's Family Paradise

The vicinity surrounding New Orleans is rich with things to do and see. Plantation homes, some restored and others in ruins, are scattered up and down the River Road, which follows the snaking curves and spirals of the Mississippi River. The nearby bayous and swamps are teeming with wildlife and vegetation. If you have an extra day or two while in New Orleans, it's well worth your while to take the family on an outing away from the city so that you see the moss-hung trees, white-columned plantations, and cypress-filled swamps that make Louisiana such a unique and interesting place.

Plantations

One of the closest plantations to New Orleans is Destrehan, which is approximately eight miles from the New Orleans International Airport. Although it is somewhat small and not ostentatious like many other plantations, Destrehan is noteworthy because it was built in 1787—making it one of the oldest plantations in the area—by a free man of color. It is built in the Greek Revival style. (504) 654-6868

Houmas House, located between Baton Rouge and New Orleans, is one of the most impressive of the restored plantations. It was used in the film *Hush, Hush, Sweet Charlotte.* Furnished with antiques, the mansion is actually two houses connected by a carriage way. There is a stunning spiral staircase that goes to the third floor and a beautiful view of the Mississippi River. (504) 473-7841

Historic Houmas House. Located on the Great River Road at Burnside, LA.
Photo by Grant L. Robertson

Located only a few minutes from Houmas House is Ashland-Belle Hélène, which was used in more movies than any other plantation. Although it is in a state of decay, it is still very interesting. Ashland-Belle Hélène is closed to the public, but there is a caretaker on the premises who might let you in to see the fascinating home where such movies as *Band of Angels*, starring Clark Gable, *The Beguiled* with Clint Eastwood, and *Long Hot Summer* with Don Johnson were filmed.

It is especially interesting to see how the home was constructed where excavation has taken place.

Another plantation in the vicinity of New Orleans is San Francisco, which is next to an oil refinery. The refinery has been responsible for restoring and maintaining the mansion. Built in 1856, the home resembles a steamboat and even boasts a belvedere in the shape of a ship's crow's nest on the third story. (504) 535-2341

Tezcuco Plantation is located seven miles above the Sunshine Bridge and has guest cottages and an antique shop. It was completed in 1855 and features columns joined by wrought-iron railings. (504) 562-3929

Probably the most spectacular of the mansions is Nottoway, which is also known as "White Castle." Built in 1859, Nottoway has sixty-four rooms and 53,000 square feet. It is also

Nottoway Plantation. *Photo by Grant L. Robertson*

the largest antebellum home in the South. Nottoway has a restaurant and overnight accommodations.
(504) 545-2409

Other plantations in the vicinity include Madewood (800) 375-7151, which is a 21-room Greek Revival home with overnight accommodations, and Ormand (504) 764-8544. Don't leave Louisiana without seeing at least one plantation home!

Swamp Tours

Have you ever wondered what it would be like to be in a swamp surrounded by alligators? You, too, can have that experience. Swamp tours are conducted in the vicinity of New Orleans daily. Most of them also give out a great deal of information and explain why swamp life is so important to the ecological system.

Alligators are often seen on the popular Louisiana Swamp Tours. *Photo by Grant L. Robertson*

The tours usually go to visit "pet" alligators and entice them with raw chicken. The alligators jump out of the water to get the meat. Be sure to bring your camera, because you won't believe your eyes! It is also wise to wear a sun hat or visor and sunglasses. It can get very hot on the boats in the summer. You will also see blue herons, wood ducks, and turtles, among other creatures. Some of the tours end up at a Cajun restaurant, where you can relax and enjoy Cajun food—including fried alligator tail.

Honey Island Swamp Tours

Organized by wetland ecologist Dr. Paul Wagner; you may spot the famous Honey Island swamp monster. Twice daily pick-ups depart from downtown New Orleans hotels. (504) 641-1769.

Tours by Isabelle

If you are looking for a small, personalized tour, call Tours by Isabelle, a company that has been serving the New Orleans area since 1979. They offer first-class city tours, plantation, and swamp tours and have thirteen passenger vans. The motto of Tours by Isabelle is "We'll make you fall in love with Louisiana!" (504) 391-3544; 888-223-2093

Steppin' Out New Orleans Tours

True Southern hospitality is the theme of Steppin' Out New Orleans Tours. The knowledgeable guides take you to the French Quarter, Garden District, cemeteries, and the estate home of Edgar and Edith Stern. If you are interested in the history of New Orleans, have a limited time to spend in the city, and dislike being herded around on a large tour, call the folks at Steppin' Out.

(504) 246-1006
A.M. Tour—$26 Adults $15 Children   9:00 A.M.-12:00 P.M.
P.M. Tour—$32 Adults $17 Children   1:00 P.M.-5:00 P.M.

Bayou Tour

Tour the bayous where Jean Lafitte and his band of pirates hid out. The Eco-Tour will take you traveling through the semitropical Barataria area, where you will experience first-hand the natural habitat of eagles, osprey, egrets, herons, ibis, pelicans, and black skimmers. This is also the migratory resting place for millions of ducks, geese, rails, snipe, and various other birds. Alligators, otters, swamp deer, and mink call these fresh and saltwater marshes home, as do fish, oysters, shrimp, and crabs.

You will ride in a deluxe 22-foot all-weather boat. The personalized tours focus on the history and ecology of one of the nation's richest estuaries. The remoteness of the area and the timing of the tours (sunrise—sunset) offer unique opportunities for wildlife observation.

————

1-800-73SWAMP; (504) 689-2911
Early bird cruise 6:00-8:00 A.M. $30
Bayou to Gulf cruise 10:00 A.M.-2:00 P.M. $45
Sunset 6:00 -8:00 P.M. (summer) $30
Sunset 3:00-5:00 P.M. (winter) $30
Six-person maximum; private charters available; refreshments and restrooms on board.

Cajun Man's Swamp Cruise

A Cajun Man's Swamp Cruise is operated by former Green Beret, State Trooper, and certified Cajun Man Ron Guidry. Fluent in French, the Cajun Man will sing you a French song while playing his guitar or accordion made from an old cedar chest. Guidry conducts his tours in the Black Bayou area, where alligators, nutria, possum, raccoons, squirrels, deer, egrets, herons, cranes, and wood ducks abound.

The Cajun Man will stop to let you pick a beautiful water hyacinth or feel the curling strands of Spanish moss hanging from the trees. Learn about the Cajun lifestyle as you glide through the bayou waters. Equipped with a cellular phone and toilet facilities, Guidry's large canopied boat is quite comfy. The Cajun Man gives special attention to the handicapped and senior citizens.

———

(504) 868-4625
E-mail: rjguidry@ampersand.net

Captain Nick's Wildlife Safaris

Saltwater and freshwater fishing are offered in the Gulf of Mexico or the inland swamps and bayous, and Captain Nick provides transportation, food and beverages, fishing licenses, and all tackle. For the more knowledgeable fishermen, fly and spinning techniques are supported and equipment is supplied.

Boats hold from one to twenty-five passengers. You may combine a fishing trip and swamp tour for the cost of a fishing trip alone. Courtesy vans, all state licensed, pick up from any New Orleans hotel. Children receive a 50 percent discount.

———

1-800-375-3474
$135 per person

Ripp's Inland Charters

If you're looking for Louisiana's best Deep South fishing adventure, Ripp Blank of Ripp's Inland Charters will fill the bill. A full day of fishing awaits you as your adventure begins by cruising down the bayou on the 21-foot *Team Avenger* powered by a 200 hp Yamaha motor.

Your guide will share some of the folklore and history of the Cajuns and pirates who have lived in these bayous over the past 250 years. Ripp, a licensed Coast Guard captain, is a lifelong resident of the town of Lafitte, located about 45 minutes south of New Orleans and named after pirate Jean Lafitte.

This maze of waterways that connects the Mississippi River to the Gulf of Mexico is full of marshes, swamps, ponds, and canals—all teeming with sea creatures. Ripp specializes in red fish and speckled trout fishing with light tackle.

For a day of adventure and fishing in the bayous, dress casually and bring an ice chest of food and drink (also used to take your cleaned fish home!). Ripp was recently featured in the *North American Fisherman* magazine. Ripp's charters start at $275 per day for two people, including rod, reel, bait, and ice. Four boats are available, and a $100 deposit is required.

———

(504) 689-2655
P.O. Box 231
Barataria, LA 70036

Trivia

Seventy-Five Fascinating Facts About the Crescent City

1. Native New Orleanians' famous New York accents are a blend of Irish and German accents.

2. New Orleans houses were often whitewashed once or twice a year, not only for looks, but also because the whitewash contained lime, which served as an insect repellent.

3. More French bread is consumed in New Orleans than in any other world city, including Paris.

4. Governor Miro in 1786 passed a decree that required all free women of color to tie up their hair and dress modestly without jewelry. This law was known as the Tignon Law. It is not uncommon today to see women of color with their hair tied up in a tignon.

5. There are three traffic lights on the Mississippi River, all located in the New Orleans area:
   Gov. Nicholls St. wharf
   Westwego
   Gretna

6. According to historian Buddy Stall, a native New Orleanian is defined as one having at least "a gross of Mardi Gras beads in his attic, a roach sighted on his premises on seven consecutive days, and his home must have been flooded at least once."

7. The first Mardi Gras queen was Mrs. Emma Butler, crowned in 1871 when she found a golden bean in her slice of king's cake (a Mardi Gras tradition).

8. New Orleans is said to have more alligators living within its city limits than any other city in the world.

9. Canal Street, which was originally laid out for a canal, never contained a canal.

10. "Neutral Ground," which is what the medians are called in New Orleans, are referred to as neutral ground because originally they separated the French from the Americans, who could not get along with each other.

11. On Good Friday, devout Catholics go to nine churches, to which they must walk. "Novena," a reference to nine days, is significant in the Catholic religion.

12. After the Civil War, General "Spoons" Butler (so named because he confiscated silver spoons) forced the sassy Frenchwomen, who had thrown slop buckets on the Union Soldiers, to clean and drain the muddy streets of New Orleans. This went on for approximately seven years during Reconstruction. There were no yellow fever epidemics in the city while the Frenchwomen cleaned the streets, but once they stopped, the dreaded epidemics started up again.

13. In St. Louis #1 Cemetery, the grave of the city's first black mayor, Ernest "Dutch" Morial, is next to that of Marie Laveau.

14. Beneath the Macy's Store at the New Orleans Center and extending underneath the parking lot of the Superdome lies the old Girod's Cemetery, the city's first Protestant burial ground. It was paved over to make room for the building of the Superdome and the shopping center.

15. New Orleans' elegant Garden District was originally part of the city of Lafayette, which included the Irish Channel neighborhood and extended all the way to the Mississippi River. Lafayette was annexed by New Orleans in 1852.

16. Since its inception, Mardi Gras has been a time to settle grudges and take revenge on one's enemy. The masks, crowds, and revelry make Carnival the perfect "payback" season. Outsiders beware! In fact, the fights became so bad between Mardi Gras Indian groups that they were not allowed to participate in the festivities for several years.

17. New Orleans' official flag (adopted in 1918) has three flues de lis and is white with blue and red borders. The golden fleurs de lis, symbolizing New Orleans' French heritage, were carried by early French explorers to Louisiana.

18. Light fixtures on Canal Street from the Mississippi to North Rampart and following North Rampart to the Municipal Auditorium are in the shape of fleurs de lis. They were a gift from Paris to New Orleans in 1930.

19. So many town leaders fought and were wounded or killed in duels that in the early 1800s, politicians were required to take an oath that they had not fought in a duel since the adoption of the state constitution.

20. Waguespack, a common New Orleans name, was originally Wagensback, a German name.

21. The first article of the original *Code Noir* (Black Code) enacted by Governor Bienville in 1724 for regulation of slaves, ordered the expulsion of all Jews from the Louisiana province. There were few Jews in New Orleans prior

to 1803, and those who chose to live there were subject to imprisonment and confiscation of property.

22. The Choctaw Indians referred to Bayou St. John as "Bayouk Choupit," meaning "bayou of mudfish (crawfish)." "Bayou" is actually an Indian word in origin. The French, who disliked consonant endings, dropped the "k" from the word.

23. Bayou St. John, which forms the western border of City Park and empties into Lake Pontchartrain, was called the "city's back door," by Bienville, early explorer and governor of Louisiana.

24. New Orleans receives approximately sixty inches of rain each year.

25. The brother of notorious criminal Jesse James, Frank, once served as the betting commissioner for the New Orleans Fairgrounds Racetrack.

26. On January 15, 1978, in true New Orleans style, King Tut, the Egyptian mummy who was being exhibited along with treasures from his ancient kingdom, received a proper sendoff in the form of a New Orleans jazz funeral parade.

27. In the 19th century, where the French Market now stands, was once the rowdy, rough area of Gallatin Street and was said by some to be as wicked as the infamous Barbary Coast of Africa.

28. Every drop of water that falls into New Orleans must be pumped out, because the city is below sea level.

29. New Orleans boasts the largest known siphon, which collects rainwater under the west side of the Industrial Canal, then carries the water underneath the canal and pumps it to Lake Borgne.

30. New Orleans natives don't go grocery shopping; they "make their groceries"—the common expression used for this task.

31. Parasols (not umbrellas) are often carried by women in New Orleans to protect them from the fierce sun.

32. The Mississippi River flows north at the foot of Canal Street, so one actually travels east to get to the west bank.

33. Years ago when most nuns wore habits, they didn't pay fare on streetcars or buses. Today they must pay, unless the Sisters are "habitually" dressed, and only the oldest nuns still wear the traditional attire.

34. Many barges that floated down the Mississippi River were unable to get back up the river, so they were broken up and their lumber sold as "barge board," which was used to build a large number of the city's shotgun houses.

35. The St. Thomas Housing Project, located in the Irish Channel neighborhood, was built in 1937 and was the nation's first public housing project. Although it was built for blacks and whites, it is now exclusively occupied by blacks.

36. Jackson Square was originally named Place d'Armes and was a military parade ground.

37. On February 17, 1899, began an unusual spectacle in New Orleans that lasted four days. For the first time in recorded history, ice chunks as large as twenty to one hundred feet in diameter floated down the Mississippi River. Crowds lined both sides of the levee to exclaim at the sight, which one spectator described as resembling a big field of dirty cotton.

38. In order to make certain there would be fresh roses blooming on the Christmas dinner table, wealthy Creole families cut rosebuds in late fall, dipped them in paraffin, wrapped them in tissue, and then placed the buds in a cool part of the house. On Christmas morning, the roses were put into hot water, and their stems were recut to allow blooming for the special event.

39. The day after Mardi Gras, Ash Wednesday, is the day Catholics go to mass and begin the observance of Lent. It is a common sight in New Orleans on Ash Wednesday to see citizens with crosses of ashes on their foreheads. The cross is made by their priest, who reminds the repentant revelers to "Remember, man, from dust thou came and to dust thou shall return."

40. Before 1958, when the Mississippi River Bridge was built, there were no hospitals in Algiers, which is across the river from New Orleans (and is in fact incorporated into the City of New Orleans). When pregnant women went into labor, they would rush to the front of the ferry waving a white handkerchief. Because so many babies ended up being born on the ferry, it was customary for the ferry to leave immediately when a pregnant woman waving a white hanky came on board.

41. Between Algiers Point and the French Quarter is the Mississippi River's deepest spot—141 feet deep.

42. In 1895 Rex, King of Mardi Gras (Frank T. Howard), became the only king to marry his queen. She was named Miss Lydia Fairchild.

43. The first American flag to fly over New Orleans (in 1803) had fifteen stars and fifteen stripes. At the time, a new star and stripe were added for each state. After the purchase of the Louisiana Territory, the practice was

changed to adding only a star for each new state and keeping thirteen stripes for the original thirteen states.

44. In the early 1880s some New Orleans tombs were decorated with tarlatan, moss, flowers, and wreaths made with seed pearls and glass beads. Some adornments were so valuable that family members sat throughout the day to guard them.

45. In the Metairie Cemetery there is a statue of a large, woolly dog, resembling a St. Bernard, beside the Masich family tomb. It seems the faithful canine followed his master's funeral procession and refused to leave the gravesite, despite extended coaxing by family members who left food for the grieving animal. Finally, the dog died and was memorialized in stone. People sometimes leave a red ribbon around the dog's neck with a card inscribed, "To a good dog."

46. The term "Dixie" originated in New Orleans before the Civil War, when river boatmen were forced to use French money on one side of Canal Street and American money on the other. Citizens Bank on Toulouse Street came to their aid by printing notes in both English and French. "Dix" means "ten" in French, and the ten-dollar notes were referred to as "Dixies." The river boatmen then began making references to "going down South to get some Dixies." The term now refers to the Deep South area in general.

47. Insults from New Orleans women directed at Union soldiers during the Civil War resulted in the infamous General Order No. 28, issued by General Benjamin "Spoons" Butler:

As the officers and soldiers of the United States have been subject to repeated insults from the women (calling themselves ladies) of New Orleans, in return for the most scrupulous noninterference and courtesy on our part, it is ordered that hereafter when any female shall, by word, gesture, or movement, insult or show contempt for any officer or soldier of the United States, she shall be regarded and held liable to be treated as a woman of the town plying her avocation.

New-Orleans, May 15, 1862

48. When the Mississippi River Bridge opened in 1958, it linked the east side with the west side, opening Algiers and other small river communities on the west bank to development.

49. Early American tradesmen who rode down the Mississippi River with their cargoes found the return trip against the mighty river a nearly impossible nightmare (before the steamboats), and most crews either walked or rode home horseback via the Natchez Trace.

50. When coffee beans became scarce during the Civil War, the citizens of New Orleans discovered that the dried and roasted root of the chicory plant made a tasty addition to the weakened brew. After the war, people continued to add chicory to their coffee, and it is still popular today.

51. When the cause of yellow fever, the *Aedis aegypti* mosquito, was discovered in 1900, the city ordered cisterns to be screened or oiled. A film of oil on the water prevented the deadly insect from breeding.

52. New Orleans has 87 miles of canals, as compared to Venice, the "City of Canals," which boasts only 28 miles.

53. The term *banquette* (a low bench) is still used for sidewalks in New Orleans and is left over from the days when wooden planks were laid on the muddy streets so ladies could walk down the street without dragging their skirts in the mire.

54. New Orleans boasts of having the largest drainage pump in the world—14 feet in diameter and able to accommodate a 2½-ton truck—designed by engineer Albert Baldwin Wood.

55. Tulane University is probably the only school with a 28-foot sailboat encased in glass on its campus. The *Nadia*, which belonged to engineer Albert Wood, is required to be displayed as a condition of Wood's will, which left a great deal of money to the university.

56. Old maps show that Tchoupitoulas Street was on the edge of the river in 1810, but it was five blocks from the river on 1840 maps. This was due to the Mississippi changing course and depositing soil from the west bank to the east bank.

57. The world's most famous streetcar, Desire, served the antique shop area along Royal Street and a section of Bourbon Street for many years and was popularized by Tennessee Williams' play *A Streetcar Named Desire*. The line was discontinued in 1948.

58. If a gris-gris (good or bad luck charm in voodoo) of wet salt in the shape of a cross is found on your porch, you will have trouble.

59. For many years it was a symbol of good housekeeping to scrub the wooden steps by your front door with powdered brick. The brick acted as a detergent on the bleached wood.

60. In 1903 a gypsy camp was established at St. Louis and Scott Streets.

61. New Orleans has produced two boxers who reached the Boxing Hall of Fame: Tony Canzoneri, a former shoe-shine boy, and Pete Herman, who went on to become a nightclub owner.

62. New Orleans City Park is so big that it has two football stadiums, four golf courses, riding trails, and scores of baseball diamonds.

63. Traditionally, Creoles were never married or buried on a Friday, because that was the day for public hangings in Place d'Armes (Jackson Square).

64. A so-called "shotgun" house is a long narrow house with front and rear doors placed so that a shot could be fired through the front and come out the back door without hitting anything. Shotgun houses were at one time very popular in New Orleans, and there are still many of them left.

65. New Orleans has the only radio station in America exclusively geared to the visually impaired, 88.3 FM, WRBH.

66. While building the fabulous Longue Vue mansion, Mr. and Mrs. Edgar Stern were dismayed to discover that one could not view the magnificent gardens planned from most places in the house. With the help of winches, cypress logs, and mules, the original house was moved and a new one built in its place. The house and gardens are open for tours to the public.

67. New Orleans' Superdome is the largest domed building in the world, surpassing Houston's Astrodome, which could easily fit inside it.

68. In 1858 New Orleans attorney S. S. Hall published *Bliss of Marriage, or How to Get a Rich Wife,* which listed all available prospective spouses in or around the city. The publication caused such an uproar that six duels were fought, and attorney Hall was forced to leave New Orleans.

69. In New Orleans the "Ladies in Red" refer to seven red and gold streetcars that make their way around the old riverfront line. One dollar and twenty-five cents will get you a one-way ride on these vintage cars.

70. Over 500,000 king cakes are sold each year in New Orleans during the Mardi Gras season, and an additional 50,000 are shipped out of state.

71. Two of the largest Carnival parades, Endymion and Bacchus, toss over 1.5 million cups, 2.5 million doubloons, and 200,000 gross of beads to excited parade-goers.

72. Tourism brings in $2 billion annually to the New Orleans economy; Mardi Gras alone brings in about $500 million.

73. The so-called Dueling Oaks in Audubon Park were the site of many duels fought between gentlemen in the olden days. In fact, the *Daily Picayune* wrote on July 29, 1837, that duels were "as common these days as watermelons."

74. José Quintero, a Cuban who lived in New Orleans, wrote a book entitled *The Code of Honor,* which explained how to react to insults and what to do when challenged.

75. Red beans and rice are traditionally served on Mondays in New Orleans. This is because Monday was wash day, and housewives needed a simple dish that could simmer all day while the clothes were laundered by hand. Large

red kidney beans cooked with onions, bell peppers, celery, and ham or andouille sausage make up this creamy, tasty New Orleans favorite. Red beans are usually served over rice with cornbread on the side. Check out the recipe in the *Food and Fun* section!

———

New Orleans Heritage: People

Indians

The first recorded group of Indians in the New Orleans area were eighteen Mohegans and Abnakis who came with the LaSalle expedition in 1681, when the explorer passed the future city site on his way to the mouth of the Mississippi. There were, however, a number of Choctaws living during this time in the lower Mississippi region, including the area that would later become New Orleans. The first official census in New Orleans in 1721 showed a total of 470 people, including 21 Indian slaves.

Flatheads and Bear Oil

The Choctaws were called "Flatheads" by the French, who were perplexed as to why the natives' heads were of an odd shape—one Frenchman, Le Page du Pratz, noting that "all the nations of Louisiana have their heads as flat, or nearly so." Du Pratz also made the following observations about Indians he made contact with in the New Orleans area:

> ...Very few of them are to be seen under five feet and a half, and very many of them above that... [T]hey are long waisted; their head is upright and somewhat flat in the upper part, and their features are regular. They have black eyes, and thick black

> hair without curls ... The men in general are better
> made than the women; they are more nervous and
> the women more plump and fleshy; the men are
> almost all large, and the women of a middle size ...
> The infants of the native are white when they are
> born, but they soon turn brown, as they are rubbed
> with bear oil and exposed to the sun.

Approximately a half-century later, a Dutch surveyor, Bernard
Romans, wrote that the Choctaw Indians "may more properly
be called a nation of farmers than any savages I have met
with." He also described why the Choctaws had flat heads:

> The women disfigure the heads of their male
> children by means of bags of sand, flattening them
> into different shapes, thinking it adds to their
> beauty.

Belle Isle and the Cannibals

Other tribes living in the vicinity included the Natchez and
Attakapas. A group of Frenchmen, headed by Monsieur de
Belle Isle, were making the treacherous voyage from France
when they reached a bay known as St. Bernard near the Gulf
of Mexico. Belle Isle took some of his men to hunt for food in
the woods and was eventually captured by the Attakapans, a
human-eating tribe. His men having died and himself near
starvation, Belle Isle threw himself on the mercy of the Indians, who decided to fatten him up and keep him as a "dog"
(slave) for an older powerful female tribal member. He stayed
with the Attakapans more than two years, learning to shoot a
bow and arrow and serving his mistress, but refusing to eat
the smoked remains of fallen enemies.

The tribe grew to trust Belle Isle, who was able to trade his
way back to the Frenchmen living at an outpost called Natchitoches after his two years of captivity. Once returned to

civilization and welcomed back by Governor Bienville himself, Belle Isle's former mistress along with a group of warriors came to visit him. Belle Isle was able to establish communications between Bienville and the Attakapans, eventually drawing up a treaty between the two groups that the tribe "leave off the barbarous custom of eating human flesh." Afterwards, Belle Isle stayed in New Orleans and assumed an official role as liaison between the governor and the tribe.

One poignant incident that is part of New Orleans history took place during the reign of Pierre Rigaud, Marquis de Vaudreuil, who began serving as governor of the region in 1743. Around 1753 a Choctaw Indian insulted a member of the Acolapissa tribe and was killed. The Acolapissa who killed him escaped to New Orleans and was pursued by the Choctaws, who insisted that the Frenchmen hand over the guilty man. The Acolapissa had by this time disappeared, and his father volunteered to give up his own life for that of his son's. The Choctaws decided this was fair, so the old warrior was taken to a fallen tree where he was killed by a tomahawk.

This episode so impressed one of the French officers, Le Blanc de Villeneuve, that he composed a play about it. *Le Père Indien* was rehearsed and presented in the Marquis de Vaudreuil's drawing room to an enthusiastic audience, becoming the first dramatic work to be presented in New Orleans.

> *In the early part of November they have an important holiday called the feast of the dead or the feast of souls. Each family gathers at the cemetery and weeps as it visits the boxes containing the bones of its ancestors. After leaving the cemetery, the Indians indulge in a great feast.*
>
> Jean-Bernard Bossu, early French colonist
> describing Indian celebration
> that resembled All Saints' Day

Creoles and French

"Creole" refers to descendants of the original French and Spanish settlers of New Orleans and also to light-skinned people of color who have mixed African, French, and/or Spanish blood. The French began exploration in the vicinity of New Orleans as early as 1682, when René-Robert Cavelier Sieur de la Salle came down the Mississippi River to a site approximately 90 miles below New Orleans and claimed all the land drained by the river for France's Sun King, Louis XIV. Explorers, often French Canadians or Spanish, continued cruising past the "beautiful crescent," as the future site of New Orleans was called by explorer Jean-Baptiste LeMoyne, Sieur de Bienville. It is the wide arc of land on the Mississippi forming "one of the most beautiful crescents of the river" (Bienville) that gave rise to one of New Orleans' popular names, the Crescent City. The area between the Mississippi and Lake Pontchartrain had long been used as a portage by Indian tribes.

Lured by False Claims

Bienville began clearing the ground for a settlement around 1718, just after Scottish financier John Law established his Company of the West (1717) for the purpose of settling the lower Mississippi Valley. Descriptions of the area were often exaggerated in printed leaflets and notices in order to lure settlers to the swampy land.

Father Charlevoix, a French priest who arrived in New Orleans in 1721, wrote the following:

> Here I am in that famous city they call New Orleans
> ... The eight hundred houses and five parishes
> which the *Mercure* attributed to it two years ago are

now reduced to a hundred huts placed without much order, to a large warehouse of wood, two or three houses which would not embellish a village in France, to half of a wretched warehouse that they have consented to assign to the Lord and of which He had hardly taken possession before they wanted Him to leave it to lodge in a tent.

Approximately 300 concessionaires with land grants came to the area in 1718 from France, with another hundred arriving the following year. Large groups of thieves, prostitutes, and other "undesirables" were shipped to Louisiana as well, as France emptied its prisons, detention houses, and hospitals into the new colony.

Writings of a Novice

In spite of the hardships of living in a new settlement, it was not long before the French established their culture, including their love of food and music. An eighteen-year-old Ursuline novice, Madeleine Hachard, arrived in New Orleans around 1728 from Rouen, France, and described the magnificent food: buffalo, wild geese, deer, turkeys, rabbits, chicken, pheasant, partridge, quail; "monstrous fish which I never knew in France"; shrimp, oysters, sweet potatoes cooked "in the ashes, like chestnuts"; a mixture of hominy, meat, and fish (likely an early form of jambalaya); figs, pumpkins, pecans, watermelons, bananas; and a drink of "much chocolate with milk and coffee."

Louisiana's Napoleonic Code

Although Spanish, Africans, Acadians, Americans, and various Europeans would populate New Orleans, the French culture retained its preeminence, as it does even today. Louisiana's Napoleonic Code, a unique system of civil and criminal law, has its origin in French law. Some of the more unusual aspects of the Code include "forced" inheritance (a father cannot disinherit his child), tort laws which are actually Roman in origin, community property in marriage (unless there is a prenuptial agreement), and responsibility of parents for the torts of minor children. The Napoleonic Code is also unique in that the judge examines each case and then applies the code to it.

The French Market, 1871 illustration. Indians, Africans, and Creoles gather at the French Market. *Historic New Orleans Collection*

New Orleans has often been referred to as "the only European city in the continental United States," and certainly the French influence is primarily responsible for the city's free-wheeling reputation. Gambling, prostitution (legal until 1917), and drinking have always been not only tolerated, but often embraced. This laissez-faire attitude led even young Madeleine Hachard to remark:

I can assure you that I do not seem to be on the Mississippi, there is as much of magnificence and politeness as in France. Cloth of gold and velours are commonplace here, albeit three times dearer than at Rouen... The women here, as elsewhere, employ powder and rouge to conceal the wrinkles in their faces; indeed, the demon here possesses a great empire.

As the French and Spanish intermarried and often sired offspring of black mistresses, the term "Creole" was broadened to include these descendants of color. "Black" Creoles tend to be very light-skinned, often have French names, and are likely to be well-to-do and hold business and community leadership positions. New Orleans is considered both a cosmopolitan and Creole city, and its Creole residents take great pride in being able to trace their ancestry to the early European and African settlers.

Africans

The earliest Africans in Louisiana were slaves brought to the territory in 1719 from the Senegambia region. At least 7,000 slaves were transported to Louisiana between 1719 and 1731 by French slavers. Slavery was very much accepted in New Orleans. A number of Africans gained their freedom and were known as "free people of color." Many of these "freemen" were educated and were the offspring of black mothers and French or Spanish settlers.

Music, Food, and Hardship

The colorful and sorrowful lives of the Africans were a central ingredient to the gumbo of New Orleans culture. In fact the word "gumbo," a spicy roux to which seafood, chicken, and/or sausage are added, is often made using okra, an African contribution to the dish. Gumbo z'herbes, another variation of gumbo, is originally a West African dish. African cooks contributed their knowledge of yams, rice, beans (red beans and rice is a popular New Orleans dish), eggplant, and garlic to many famous New Orleans dishes.

Along with their culinary knowledge, African settlers brought their native music and spiritism in the form of the Voodoo religion. Congo Square (now Louis Armstrong Park), near the French Quarter, was long the gathering place for slaves and free people of color, particularly on weekends when the Square became the site of exotic ritual tribal dances and celebrations.

Slave Dances at Congo Square

The slave dances at Congo Square were a unique attraction for visitors to New Orleans. Author Herbert Asbury describes one such gathering in his book *The French Quarter*:

> The favorite dances of the slaves were the Calinda, a variation of which was also used in the Voodoo ceremonies, and the Dance of the Bamboula, both of which were primarily based on the primitive dances of the African jungle, but with copious borrowings from the *contra-danses* of the French … [T]he male dancers attached tin or other metal to ribbons tied about their ankles. Thus accoutered, they pranced back and forth, leaping into the air and stamping in unison, occasionally shouting "Dansez Bomboula! Badoum! Badoum!" while the women, scarcely lifting their feet from the ground, swayed their bodies from side to side and chanted

ancient song... [T]he entire square was an almost
solid mass of black bodies stamping and swaying to
the rhythmic beat of the bones upon the cask, the
frenzied, chanting of the women, and the clanging
of the pieces of metal which dangled from the
ankles of the men.

The African instruments, such as drum and banjo, and songs
eventually gave rise to street bands and later to jazz. After a
time the gatherings in Congo Square caused so much concern
among New Orleans citizens, who feared slave uprisings, that
in 1817 they were limited to Sunday daylight hours only.

THE BAMBOULA.

Dancing the Bamboula in Congo Square. Magazine illustration, 1886.
Historic New Orleans Collection

The *Code Noir*

All was not music and celebration for Africans, of course, whose lives consisted of slave auctions and hard tortuous labor. There were so many slaves in Louisiana when Bienville was governor that he enacted the infamous *Code Noir* to subjugate slaves. Based on laws of Santo Domingo, the regulations required harsh penalties for any slave found guilty of causing an uprising, and branding, mutilation, or death for slaves who stole, ran away, or struck a white person. The Code forbade interracial marriages and prohibited slaves from owning property or carrying weapons.

On a positive note, the Black Code required masters to feed and clothe their slaves properly and allow them "freedom" on Sundays and Holy Days. Masters were also required to

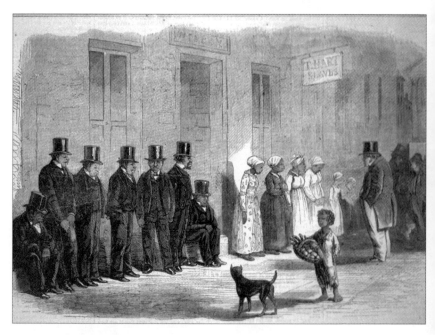

A slave pen in New Orleans. *Historic New Orleans Collection*

provide instruction in Roman Catholicism. Freed slaves were granted "the same rights, privileges, and immunities that are enjoyed by free-born persons. It is our pleasure that their merit in having acquired their freedom shall produce in their favor, not only with regard to their persons, but also to their property, the same effects which our other subjects derive from the happy circumstance of their having been born free."

Emancipation

After the abolition of slavery at the time of the Civil War, Negro aid societies, called "Social Aid and Pleasure Clubs," were formed to provide parades, entertainment, civic work, and even funeral services to members. Still in existence today, these SA & PCs are credited with originating the famous New Orleans jazz funeral parades. They are also very active in Mardi Gras festivities and provide important social support to the black communities.

As previously mentioned, from the beginning of the establishment of New Orleans, free people of color existed in the colony. One of the most infamous and powerful free African women of old New Orleans was voodoo queen Marie Laveau, whose potent black magic caused even the mention of her name to fill grown men with terror.

There were also many free blacks who moved to New Orleans from the West Indies. These people of color developed their own society independent of the African slaves. New Orleans is famous for its diversity and acceptance of all races. New Orleans' first black mayor, Ernest "Dutch" Morial, was elected in 1977. African-Americans have grown in political power and clout as the city has grown and, as cofounders of New Orleans, are an essential part of the mixture of lively times in the Crescent City.

Spanish

Spanish rule in Louisiana dates from 1762, when Louis XV of France deeded the territory to his cousin the King of Spain, Charles III, by the secret Treaty of Fountainbleau. Spanish survivors of Hernando de Soto's expedition had floated past the future site of New Orleans around 1643, as did other Spanish parties during the era. The region was originally claimed for the King of France, however, and when it was surreptitiously handed over to the Spanish, New Orleanians were not happy. Prominent citizens met and drew up a petition urging King Louis XV to rescind his treaty.

Bloody O'Reilly

It was not until 1766 that the first Spanish governor, Antonio de Ulloa, arrived in New Orleans. The unpopular ruler was eventually driven away in 1768, after the city's merchants and planners called for his expulsion. Spain did finally assert its rule in Louisiana when General Alejandro O'Reilly (referred to as "Bloody" O'Reilly due to his unpopular and sometimes tyrannical ways) arrived accompanied by an armada of twenty-four ships. Twenty-six hundred Spanish troops marched down the gangplanks and over to the Place d'Armes, where the French flag was taken down and replaced by the crimson and gold flag of Bourbon Spain. O'Reilly ordered the arrest of twelve men who led the revolt against Ulloa. Five men died in the ensuing scuffle, and six were ordered hanged. When no hangman could be found, the men were shot the following day.

O'Reilly made changes in the French governing system as well, substituting Spanish laws for the French ones, organizing a Spanish Cabildo (municipal court), and improving New Orleans' militia and public structures. The present-day

Cabildo, adjacent to St. Louis Cathedral, is a remnant of the days of Spain's rule. The building, which housed the Spanish council, was begun in 1795 and was not completed until after the Americans came to power in 1803.

For the most part, New Orleans prospered under Spanish rule, and the population grew tremendously. O'Reilly was succeeded by General Don Esteban Rodriguez Miro, who was followed by François Louis Hector, Baron de Carondelet (1792).

Spanish Architecture and Influence in New Orleans

Two fires, one in 1788 and the other in 1795, destroyed much of the original city built by the French. The destruction greatly altered the city's appearance and introduced Spanish-style architecture to the city. Under the leadership of Carondelet, all buildings over one story in the main part of the city had to be constructed of adobe or brick and have tile roofs. Night watchmen began patrolling the streets under the new oil street lamps installed at corners.

It was during this time also that the charming, intricately detailed wrought-iron balconies began to appear in New Orleans. One of the more famous wrought-iron structures may be seen at 915 Royal Street. Known as the Cornstalk Fence, a doctor had it built for his wife in the 1850s, who was homesick for the cornfields of her native Midwest.

The Spanish also popularized the addition of tomatoes, green peppers, and their own spices to the rich French food. Shrimp Creole, a tomato, green pepper, onion, and shrimp dish served over rice is of Spanish origin.

At a famous dinner on April 12, 1803, James Monroe began negotiating the purchase of the Louisiana territory from

France. Of course, France had to first get the property back from Spain, which they did on November 30, 1803, at the Cabildo. On December 20 of the same year, the Louisiana territory was officially sold to the United States for approximately $15 million. By the time the Spaniards left, New Orleans' population had more than doubled, increasing to over 8,000 people during their reign.

Germans

Although their names and culture were absorbed by the French settlers of early New Orleans, the German immigrants played an important role in New Orleans history. Between 1718 and 1724, several thousand Germans (estimates vary between 2,600 and 10,000) left their homes for Louisiana after reading greatly exaggerated descriptions of the land "filled with gold, silver, copper, and lead mines."

The German Coast

Even though hundreds did not survive the passage, so many settled in the New Orleans area that the heavily wooded region north of the city along the riverbank became known as the German Coast. These hearty pioneers cleared the wilderness, farmed, built houses, and married French girls, who named their children Anatole or Marcel, rather than Fritz, Hans, or Otto.

The blond, blue-eyed industrious settlers rowed down the Mississippi on Sunday mornings to sell their produce in front of the churches. It is said that German produce twice saved the city from famine.

Pierre Clément de Laussat, a French diplomat, wrote of the Germans in the 1740s: "What is called here the 'German

Coast' is the most industrious, the most populous, the most at ease, the most upright, the most respected part of the inhabitants of this colony."

Other travelers of the era wrote of the Germans' neat little white houses in "endless numbers" on both banks of the Mississippi. The settlers' names, such as Wichner, Toxler, and Himmel, were altered by French priests to Vicknair, Trosclair, and Hymel. Many Germans in the city settled in the area between Elysian Fields and Esplanade Avenue, which became known as "Little Saxony."

View of downriver side of Esplanade Avenue looking toward the lake from the corner of Royal Street, c. 1860. *Historic New Orleans Collection*

Today few traces of these pioneers remain; there is the nearby town of Des Allemands and the occasional German name, such as Adler's Jewelry, Leidenheimer's Bakery, and Kolb's

Restaurant on St. Charles Avenue. Many citizens remember Jax Brewery, founded in 1890 by Laurance Fabacher, which is no longer in operation.

After 1914 Germans often concealed their ancestry, particularly as anti-German sentiment increased. However, the Deutsches Haus, founded in 1928, remains active in the preservation of German culture in New Orleans. Each October the festival of Oktoberfest celebrates German food, drink, and dance.

————

Deutsches Haus—(504) 522-8014

Acadians (Cajuns)

Perhaps the most poignant and powerful stories of immigration to Louisiana involved the Acadians, or Cajuns, as they are known today. The Acadians were French people who settled in Canada in the early 1600s in a province known as Acadia and now called Nova Scotia. These French-speaking people lived quiet, isolated lives for a hundred years, until 1754, during the French and Indian War, when the British demanded that the Acadians pledge allegiance to England and renounce their Catholic religion.

Pride and Persecution of the Cajuns

The Acadians, who refused to give up their heritage and beliefs, were then rounded up by the British and deported; some were sold as servants to Americans, others were sent to concentration camps in England, and many were returned to France. Some managed to escape and hide in Nova Scotia. During this persecution, families were separated, often never to see each other again. Longfellow's famous poem

"Evangeline" is a tale of an Acadian maiden searching in Louisiana for her lost love.

The Acadians began arriving in Louisiana around 1763, often coming from France, and eventually comprised one of the largest transatlantic migrations in American colonial history. More than 1,600 of the displaced Acadians came to Louisiana between May and December 1785, after hearing of the Spanish government's (who were ruling Louisiana at that time) promises of land, seed, tools, livestock, and free transportation to the Louisiana territory.

Although they disembarked at New Orleans, the Acadians settled mostly in southwestern Louisiana, in the Lafayette area, where they continued isolated lives fishing, hunting, and trapping in the swamps. Nicknamed "Cajuns," these settlers were far different from the Creole French with their culture and refined ways. Cajuns spoke a dialect of French that includes words from African and Indian languages and is still spoken today in Louisiana's Cajun country. The Cajuns contributed a unique way of life, such as spicy food and zydeco music, which is celebrated every year at Cajun festivals that bring people from around the world to experience and enjoy the famous culture of the proud Cajun people. Today, at least half a million Louisianians claim to have Acadian ancestry.

Americans

The "wild Kaintucks," as they were called by the Creoles, began regularly floating down the river during the governorship of Bernardo de Gàlvez (1776-1785). They came from the Ohio Valley on flatboats loaded with produce. These tough American frontiersmen disturbed the refined culture of the Creoles with their bad manners and rambunctious ways. The Americans, on the other hand, knew a superior culture and shipping route when they saw it and soon set about acquiring New Orleans for the United States.

Spain had retroceded New Orleans to Napoleon, and in 1803 Thomas Jefferson was able to secure the entire Louisiana Territory, including free use of the Mississippi River. The territory was over 900,000 square miles and was one-third of the present United States. Jefferson appointed William C. C. Claiborne as the first governor of Louisiana.

The Creoles vs. the Wild Kaintucks

In the meantime, New Orleanians received word that their beloved city was about to pass into American hands. Not surprisingly, there was a great deal of unhappiness and resistance to the change, and for generations afterward the relations between Creoles and Americans were marked by strain and antagonism.

The 28-year-old governor reported to President Jefferson that the people of Louisiana were "uninformed, indolent, luxurious—in a word, ill-fitted to be useful citizens of a Republic." Governor Claiborne also made the following observations about the Creoles:

> I have seen, Sir, in this city, many youth to whom nature has been apparently liberal, but from the injustice and inattention of their parents, have no accomplishments to recommend them but dancing with elegance and ease. The same observation will apply to the young females, with this additional remark, that they are among the most handsome women in America.

Americans moved to New Orleans in increasing numbers and settled in the Faubourg Ste. Marie area, which became distinctly different from the old Creole section of the city. The

Yankees built three-storied brick houses reminiscent of New England colonial homes. Even though the Creoles remained aloof to the Americans for a number of years, the enthusiastic commercial pursuits and city developments of the new settlers eventually drew all the inhabitants of New Orleans together.

Americans established the city's first Protestant church in 1805. Louisiana was admitted to the Union April 30, 1812, with New Orleans as the capital city. The beautiful Garden District, which extends from Jackson to Louisiana Avenue between St. Charles Avenue and Magazine Street, is a particularly charming section of old New Orleans and was originally settled by prosperous Americans who built their Georgian and Greek Revival mansions behind thick palms, live oaks, and luscious magnolias.

Irish

By the year 1850 one out of every five New Orleans residents was Irish. Although many Irish had come to New Orleans through France and Spain, thousands of refugees entered the port in the mid-1840s during the Irish potato famine. Early Irish settlers who married Creoles were called "lace-curtain Irish" and were far different from their poor, starving fellow countrymen who arrived during the famine. The latter group, having no money, were forced to remain in New Orleans, where they went to work digging canals and doing other tasks usually considered too dangerous for slaves.

The Irish refugees settled in riverfront sections above and below Jackson Avenue that became known as the "Irish Channel," and in the district between New Basin and Canal Street, extending down Tulane Avenue to Broad Street. By 1880, of the total 41,157 foreign-born inhabitants, the German and

Irish made up three-fourths (17,639 Germans and 14,018 Irish). The total city population was 216,090.

Irish Pride, Hardship, and Culture

The first-generation Irish pioneers unfortunately did not carry resistance to diseases found in the swamps, and many died of yellow fever, cholera, and other diseases. Three cemeteries, known as Saint Patrick's Cemeteries, are located at Canal and City Park Avenue and contain the remains of these industrious settlers.

The Irish endured not only swamp fevers, but prejudice from Creole and American residents. It was not easy to leave the clean water and green valleys of Ireland for the bayous of Louisiana. The great-grandfather of actor Tyrone Power, a ruddy Irishman who emigrated to Louisiana, described the conditions of his fellow working Irishmen as laboring under a sun "at times insufferably fierce, and amidst a pestilential swamp whose exhalations were fetid to a degree scarcely endurable even for a few minutes . . . wading amongst stumps of trees, mid-deep in black mud, clearing the spaces pumped out by powerful steam engines."

Even though the Irish were sometimes notorious for fighting and hot tempers, they assimilated into local culture, entering politics and celebrating their heritage with a huge St. Patrick's Day parade each March. Today the Irish tradition is kept alive by such locals as Danny O'Flaherty, a singer and owner of O'Flaherty's Irish Channel Pub in the French Quarter.

———

O'Flaherty's
514 Toulouse St. 70130
(504) 529-4570

See *Margaret Haughery*

Italians

New Orleans' mild climate and easy lifestyle were a magnet for another group of European immigrants, the Italians. One of the first Italians in Louisiana was Enrico Tonti, who came with the LaSalle expedition in 1682. By 1890 the total number of Italians in New Orleans was 3,622. The Italian immigration picked up around the turn of the century and continued until after World War I.

Spaghetti in the French Quarter

Most of the immigrants came from Sicily and settled in the French Quarter, which had fallen into decay after the French began moving to surrounding areas. The Italians were fruit marketers, shoemakers, and grocers, and they lived in rundown houses and crumbling mansions partitioned into a multitude of rooms. Their love of food and wine blended well with the New Orleans traditions, and soon there were rows of garlic and spaghetti hanging from courtyards in the Quarter.

New Orleans Mafia

There was, however, a dark side to the Italian community, which represented only a fraction of the immigrants but affected all of them. In the late 1800s, on occasion, an Italian was found murdered—usually a Sicilian. There began to be rumors of a New Orleans Mafia, which spread as Sicilian Mafia members fled Italy and settled in New Orleans.

Fear grew among Italian merchants, and alarming shots began to shatter the former quiet of courtyards. New Orleans officials for the most part were apathetic and reasoned that as long as the Sicilians killed each other, it was all right.

The growing Mafia scare heated up in October 1890. There had been an ongoing dispute between the Provezano and Matranga families over control of banana loaders. New Orleans Police Chief David Hennessey, who was friendly with the Provezanos, intervened on their behalf. On his way home one night, Hennessey was ambushed and murdered by a group of Italians.

A committee was formed to investigate the crime, and charges were brought against twenty men. Feelings in the city ran high against the accused; some were beaten in prison during the long trial. Even though the state had a strong case, stories of jury tampering circulated, and when the verdicts of not guilty came down for some and mistrials for others, the city was in an uproar. It was Friday, March 13, 1891.

As fate would have it, two shiploads of 1,800 Italian immigrants had just arrived. Their untimely entrance, combined with the rejoicing and celebration of the Italian community over the verdicts, caused anti-Italian sentiment to explode. The day following the verdict, the paper called for "all good citizens" to meet on Canal Street "to take steps to remedy the failure of justice."

An angry mob assembled at the old Congo Square and proceeded to hunt down eleven men. As the manhunt began, terrified Italians fled their homes and hid in toolsheds and homes of sympathetic non-Italians. One woman told of taking in an Italian woman who begged, "Save-a me, please! Save-a my chil'ren!"

The eleven men were found and pumped with bullets as they begged for mercy. Two were dragged out to trees and hung. This ugly episode made international news and resulted in the withdrawal of the U.S. Italian minister and a statement by President Benjamin Harrison that the killings were "deplorable and discreditable...an offense against law and humanity."

Although the incident left the Italian community scarred, the vast majority, who were law-abiding citizens, soon recovered. Today Italian culture is found in New Orleans markets, bakeries, and ice cream shops. St. Joseph's Day, a holiday observing the delivery of Sicilians from famine, is celebrated every March 19. St. Joseph altars, which consist of dozens of Sicilian dishes such as stuffed artichokes and pasta Milanese, are prepared all over the city. A parade is also held during the holiday. For more information on Italian culture in New Orleans, visit the Italian-American Renaissance Foundation Museum.

―――――

Italian-American Renaissance Foundation Museum
537 St. Peter
(504) 891-1904

Famous and Infamous New Orleanians

Jean Lafitte (circa 1780-1826)

Perhaps the most legendary and romantic figure in New Orleans lore, Jean Lafitte first appeared in the city with his brother Pierre around 1806. A great deal of legend, tradition, speculation, and literature surround his memory. Some say Lafitte was a villain, a pirate, and a murderer, while others believe he was a gentleman smuggler, a patriot, and a privateer. The places and times of his birth and death are greatly disputed, although he was born in France and likely died on an island off the coast of Yucatan.

Jean and Pierre Lafitte opened a blacksmith shop on St. Philip Street and later a store on Royal Street. Both operations were fronts for the smuggling the two were doing. Not long after their arrival in New Orleans, the brothers were residing in a mansion at Bourbon and St. Philip Streets. The two entertained often in their mansion and charmed their way to prominence in the city.

Barataria Hideaway

The smugglers set up their illegal business in Grand Terre near Barataria Bay, where ships entered and exited the Mississippi River, and it was here that they kept their operations running for a decade. The two became involved with slave smuggling, and on occasion, up to 400 slaves a day were smuggled into Louisiana and later sold at auction. Pierre Lafitte displayed slaves and took orders for them at his shop on Royal Street. Some prospective buyers even went to Grand Terre to buy their slaves.

The Pirates and the Governor

Sources report that Lafitte's smuggling operation from Barataria was so successful that by 1813 most of New Orleans stores were being supplied with the pirated merchandise. During that year Governor William C. C. Claiborne condemned the Baratarians as pirates and warned merchants to quit dealing with them. The governor's proclamation had the reverse of its intended effect on the Lafitte brothers, who returned to the city, took out ads in the newspaper announcing sales of merchandise, and began hosting a series of lavish dinners and parties for merchants. When the beleaguered governor posted a five-hundred-dollar reward for the arrest and delivery of Jean Lafitte, Lafitte responded by posting in prominent places a fifteen-hundred-dollar reward for the arrest and delivery of Governor Claiborne to Grand Terre. This action resulted in a grand jury indictment against the Lafittes and other Baratarians for piracy. Pierre ended up serving several months in jail until he mysteriously broke out.

War of 1812

During the War of 1812 (in the year 1814), Governor Claiborne sent the U.S. Navy to destroy Lafitte's Grand Terre establishment. The navy took the pirates by surprise, capturing nine ships and a hundred prisoners, including Dominique You, one of the more renowned pirates of Lafitte's band and a former soldier (see *Cities of the Dead*). Jean and Pierre managed to escape the attack by disappearing into the surrounding bayous.

Jean Lafitte was not to be conquered. A few days before the attack against him, a British ship commander had approached the pirate and offered him thirty thousand dollars in gold to aid his troops in an attack on New Orleans. Lafitte got as many details as he could about the British plans and then went to the governor with the information, offering to join the Americans in repelling the invasion. Despite the destruction of Lafitte's settlement, he insisted on helping with the war effort, and General Andrew Jackson inducted the two brothers, Dominique You, and the captured pirates into the American army, in exchange for dropping the charges against them. Jean Lafitte and his pirate band were afterwards commended by Jackson for their bravery, courage, and fidelity during the Battle of New Orleans.

Outcast

After the war, Lafitte felt somewhat tainted by his experience and by continued references to him as "Lafitte the pirate." Along with Pierre and their men, he went to Port-au-Prince to settle but was compelled to leave by the governor there. For three years the pirates wandered the Gulf of Mexico seeking a place to establish operations and seizing vessels on occasion.

Eventually, in 1816, the pirate band settled on an island off the Texas coast, which they called "Galvez-town." It later became the city of Galveston. Lafitte and his pirates prospered here for several years, even becoming involved with Spanish revolutionary movements in Texas and Mexico.

The colony became a refuge for vicious criminals and fugitives from justice. In 1819 Lafitte's group was involved in an attack on a Spanish vessel in the Gulf of Mexico, which resulted in the arrest and execution of seventeen of his men.

In 1821 an American warship anchored at Galvez-town, and the captain informed Lafitte that he had three months to evacuate the island. At the end of three months, the brig returned to find Lafitte supervising the settlement's destruction. Fire was set to the place, and Lafitte sailed out of the harbor with his men and three ships.

Until the end of his life (circa 1826), the man known as "the Terror of the Gulf" practiced smalltime piracy and thievery. Jean Lafitte supposedly died of a fever in a little Indian village, Teljas, off the coast of Yucatan.

Lafitte's Blacksmith Shop, located at 941 Bourbon Street, is said to be the shop out of which the brothers sold their smuggled goods. Although the building dates back to 1772 and was built using timber and soft brick (an early type of construction), no one knows where the Lafitte brothers' blacksmith shop was actually located. The old building now houses a popular New Orleans bar.

Micaela de Pontalba—*The Fiery Red-Haired Baroness*

Her father was Don Andres Almonester y Roxas, a controversial Spanish developer and philanthropist who gave money to build St. Louis Cathedral and other public institutions. Her mother was Louise de La Ronde, who married the Don when he was sixty-two and she was twenty-nine years old. She was Micaela Almonester y Roxas, and, like her prominent father, she was fiery and headstrong from an early age.

Born in New Orleans in 1795, Micaela was educated at the Ursuline Convent and was married to her cousin, Joseph Xavier Celestin Delfau de Pontalba, at age fifteen. The arranged marriage to "Tin-Tin," as his family called him, was full of troubles. By the time his daughter married, the Don had died, Louise had remarried, and she was looking for a wealthy French boy to marry Micaela and increase the family fortune.

Tin-Tin lived in France with his family, and his father, the Baron de Pontalba, had been a nobleman under Napoleon's rule. Micaela's future husband had traveled to Louisiana with his mother to meet his red-haired cousin, and Louise had her attorneys draw up a marriage contract. The wedding of Micaela and Celestin was spectacular, with a procession moving from the Almonester home on the Place d'Armes to the imposing Spanish-style cathedral. There were silk, diamonds, and flowers. It seemed to be a match made in the stars.

The couple sailed to Europe, where they lived quietly for several years and had three sons. It soon became evident, however, that Micaela was bored with family life and most of all with her soft-spoken husband, who enjoyed spending his evenings embroidering at home. Meanwhile, her father-in-law, Baron de Pontalba, had expected to acquire the Almonester fortune, since Micaela was the Don's only living child. The baron found that Louise had given her daughter control over much of the property, even though she was married. Baron de Pontalba was also angry that Louise had received much more from the estate than had Micaela. There grew to be an intense dislike between Micaela and the baron, who was to discover he had met his match in his willful daughter-in-law.

Extravagant Lifestyle

Micaela, meanwhile, saw herself as a queen in the world of society and insisted on acquiring jewels and fine clothes and living extravagantly. Her husband provided his wife with the best of everything, even though the Pontalba fortune was quickly dwindling. As the baron became increasingly distraught over Micaela's spending habits, Micaela threatened to sue her own mother for a larger share of her father's estate. A new settlement was drawn up that gave Micaela valuable properties in New Orleans facing the Place d'Armes. There were several more years of luxurious gifts, numerous servants, and patronizing the arts. A wealthy baroness, Micaela reasoned, should live like one.

Now that his wife had taken control of things, Tin-Tin grew unhappy and eventually left to go live with his father. He wrote Micaela that she had ceased to love or respect him and that he would work to overcome his weakness and become master of the domain. The couple reunited and went to live in their own house in Paris, away from Tin-Tin's father and mother. The baroness furnished the house with elaborate mirrors and inlaid woods and set things up for lavish entertaining. Once again, Tin-Tin complained of feeling like a stranger in his own home.

Micaela continued giving parties, and in 1826 her mother died, leaving the entire Almonester fortune to the Baroness de Pontalba. There were fights between Micaela, her husband, and the baron over property rights, payments, and all of the new arrangements. Tin-Tin soon left his wife again and went to New Orleans to check out the properties. Micaela followed him shortly, visiting her attorneys and demanding a divorce. When the Pontalbas learned of her action, they appealed to the French government. Eventually, the divorce plan was rejected.

Trouble in France

Returning to France, Tin-Tin seized his wife's properties over there and won a court order commanding Micaela to come home. His stubborn wife defied the court order and instead took a trip around America, even arranging to be introduced to President Andrew Jackson. Although the baroness owned three chateaux in France, she insisted she had become a "Jackson Democrat." When Micaela returned to Paris, her home was padlocked. She went to where her husband was staying in another part of France and was forced to room in the guest cottage. This time, it was Micaela who left Tin-Tin.

In 1834 a problem developed with one of their grown sons, and Micaela went to visit her husband to discuss it. She ended up staying the night, only to be confronted in her bedroom the next morning by an angry Baron de Pontalba, who pointed two pistols at his daughter-in-law. The furious old man shot her several times: in the shoulder; in the hand, tearing off one finger; and in the breast, where the bullet remained the rest of the baroness' life. The baron then shot himself in the head, blowing his brains out. A terrified Tin-Tin ran up the stairs and came upon the horrible scene.

Micaela recovered, but she suffered from fainting spells the rest of her life. The Paris newspapers ran stories of the incident for weeks. The Creole baroness returned to her life of parties, buying a palace originally built by Louis XIV for the Duc du Maine. In 1848 there was a revolution in France, and Micaela returned to her native New Orleans. Possibly the single biggest taxpayer in the city, Micaela decided to do something about her properties. She noted that the French section of the city was badly neglected, and the Americans were taking over in their architectural style.

New Orleans Properties

The baroness hired famed architect James Gallier to build two side-by-side buildings that replaced the run-down ones in the Place d'Armes. Micaela watched over every detail of the Renaissance-style buildings decorated with continuous ironwork reaching to the third stories. The dwelling units were among the first, if not the first, of their kind in America. The bottom stories were to be used for shops, and families would live above in magnificent living quarters. Each building had sixteen apartments with balconies, chandeliers, marble fireplaces, rosewood furnishings, and interior courts. Entwined at regular intervals in the ironwork were the letters "A" and "P," for Almonester and Pontalba. A fourth story was built for servants' quarters. The Pontalba Buildings, as they were known, quickly became an exclusive address in New Orleans.

Next Micaela looked to the Place d'Armes and decided it was in need of a complete makeover. She had the century-old oaks chopped down and replaced them with formal plantings and curving walls. Micaela renamed the area "Jackson Square" and commissioned a sculpture of the admired military leader and former president. The famous sculpture of Jackson on his horse rearing its hind legs has withstood hurricanes and booming cannons for over a hundred years.

Baroness de Pontalba returned to Paris after her civic improvements. Her husband lived awhile longer, and the two continued to meet at social occasions. She lived until the age of seventy-nine, going to parties until her final days.

Sculpture of Andrew Jackson in Jackson Square. *Photo by Grant L. Robertson*

The famous Pontalba Apartments, flanked by Jackson Square, have classic New Orleans charm with their ironwork, green shutters, and creamy white woodwork. Today the Pontalba Apartments are still an exclusive address in New Orleans.

———

See *Pontalba Buildings, Jackson Square*

Margaret Haughery (1813-1882)

At the age of nine, she became an orphan when her Irish parents, Margaret O'Rourke and William Gaffney, succumbed to a yellow fever epidemic. Her husband, Charles Haughery, died of consumption when she was only twenty-two, and she found her baby daughter Frances dead in her crib only a few weeks later.

Her name was Margaret Gaffney Haughery, and hardship and loneliness defined her young life. Unable to read or write, she was left alone in New Orleans, where she had moved from Baltimore in 1835 for her husband's health. Margaret was born in 1813 near Killeshandra, Co. Caven (Ireland) and moved to Baltimore with her parents and two siblings in 1818. After her parents and a baby sister died, Margaret and her brother were separated, and she was raised by a woman named Mrs. Richards.

Coping with Death

Following the untimely deaths of her husband and baby daughter, a priest, Father Mullen, befriended the young widow, and tried to help her find a way to support herself. All she wanted to do, she told the priest, was "hold a babe in me arms." For a while, Margaret worked as a laundress, until one evening she was taken by Father Mullen to visit the Poydras Asylum, an orphanage on Julia Street run by Catholic nuns. When Margaret saw the forty or so girls lined up to greet her and then soothed a baby to sleep, she cried with pleasure and begged the Sisters to allow her to work for them in exchange for room and board. Many of the children had lost their parents during a recent yellow fever epidemic.

Although she could have become a nun, Margaret chose not to because she felt she needed to move about freely in the world to assist the children. The feisty young woman went to work right away, first securing a loan from Father Mullen to purchase two cows to provide milk for the children. It was the first of many loans she would acquire and pay back in her lifetime.

The next day she visited the French Market and talked to some of the Irish merchants, who generously agreed to donate older produce and even flour, meat, and chickens for the "wee bairns." Soon Margaret and her Negro assistant were standard fixtures in the French Quarter, using wheelbarrows or sometimes a dray to haul their collections home.

The New Orphanage

When the Poydras Asylum was turned over to the Presbyterians to run, Margaret found a dilapidated "haunted" old house, known as "Old Withers" at 169 New Levee Street, and convinced the owner, a Judge Kennedy, to let the girls live there rent-free, in exchange for repairing the place. With the help of young men from St. Patrick's Church, the Sisters of Charity moved in with Margaret and the girls in 1836. Neighbors and friends donated furnishings, clothing, money, and food to the orphanage. There were soon 134 orphans living at the house on New Levee Street.

In 1838 the Sisters received the happy news that a local widow, Madame Therese Perie Saulet, had left a square of property bounded by Clio, Erato, Prytania, and Coliseum to "build all structures necessary to establish a haven or asylum for Catholic orphans." After months of selling surplus milk and sponsoring fundraisers, $36,000 had been raised, and an architect was hired to build the orphanage at 1404 Clio Street. The Sisters, Margaret, and 109 orphaned children moved into their new home February 16, 1840, which was named the New Orleans Female Orphan Asylum. It was also known as the Camp Street Asylum. By this time, the two cows purchased by Margaret had grown to a herd of forty, kept and tended by dairymen in an uptown area.

Yellow Fever Strikes

In 1853 the city was swept by its worst yellow fever epidemic. Fifty thousand of New Orleans' 150,000 residents left town, and of those remaining, approximately one in ten died. All the available Sisters of Charity and Margaret soon began spending their days nursing the sick and dying at the Charity Hospital. The misery of people on filthy cots spread on the lawn, tugging at the women's skirts was almost more than Margaret could bear. It brought back painful memories of her own mother and father's deaths from the fever.

Amazingly, none of the original children in the orphanage came down with the disease, possibly having developed immunities during earlier epidemics. Many New Orleans parents died, and the orphanage took in more children to care for. Some 209 children were admitted to the asylum during that fateful summer.

A Legacy of Charity

After a long illness, Margaret Haughery died February 9, 1882, at the age of sixty-nine years. At the time of her death, she had become owner of a bakery and no longer lived at the orphanage, although she had remained very involved in its support. Her funeral, attended by thousands of mourners, was led by the mayor and included two former governors of Louisiana as pallbearers.

The *Daily Picayune* printed the following editorial comment on the day following her death: "She never had upon her hand a kid glove, she never wore a silk dress, though she earned by hard labor many thousands of dollars. But no woman has been borne to the tomb within the limits of New Orleans who was more generally respected and loved."

It was estimated that she left half a million dollars to care for the orphans and poor. All the city's offices and stores closed the day of her funeral. Margaret was buried in St. Louis Cemetery No. 2, then later moved to St. Louis No. 3 after her tomb was destroyed by a hurricane.

A statue in Margaret's honor sculpted by Alexander Doyle was unveiled in 1884, complete with her trademark shawl and a

Statue of Margaret Haughery. *Historic New Orleans Collection*

small girl at her side. The likeness was placed in the tiny "Margaret Park," set against the backdrop of the New Orleans Female Orphan Asylum.

In 1988 experts cleaned and repaired the statue, by then badly decayed due to "sugaring" and acid rain, which resulted in mossy growth in its crevices. Now surrounded by landscaping, her inscription simply reads "Margaret," but in the words of Governor Nicholls, the woman herself is best described.

> The substance of her life was charity; the spirit of it, truth, the strength of it, religion; and the end, peace—then fame and immortality.

Kate Chopin (1850-1904)

The acclaimed author of the controversial novel *The Awakening*, Katherine O'Flaherty Chopin was born in 1850 to Eliza and Thomas O'Flaherty in St. Louis. Her French and Irish upbringing would prepare her to adapt well to the New Orleans culture where she would find her writing voice. Kate's father, a self-made man and civic leader, was killed during a bridge collapse when Kate was only five years old.

Kate O'Flaherty grew up in a household of independent women (most of whom were widows), learning French, piano, reading and writing, and how to survive in the world without a man. After living through harrowing adventures in the Civil War (her mother was forced at bayonet point to hoist the Union flag), Kate graduated from the Sacred Heart Academy in St. Louis in 1868 and became popular in local society, where she was known for her love of dancing and her talk of women's rights.

Marriage and Move to Louisiana

In 1870 Kate married Oscar Chopin, who was born in Louisiana in 1844, and the two went on a European honeymoon. The Chopins soon settled in the Garden District (1413-1415 Louisiana Avenue) in New Orleans, and Kate produced five sons. Oscar's cotton business began failing, and he moved his large family to a farm in Cloutierville, a tiny town near Natchitoches. A daughter, Lélia, was born there.

In Cloutierville, Kate shocked residents with her lavender riding habits and feathered hats, her casual display of ankles, and her fondness for Cuban cigarettes. Oscar Chopin contracted malaria and died in 1882, leaving Kate with six children and $12,000 of debt. She sold some property, ran the plantation, managed the family store, and in general took charge of her life. She also received help and advice from a neighbor whose relationship with Kate was another source of scandal in her young life.

Early Writings

After several years as a widow with a brood of children, a physician suggested that Kate write about her experiences in Louisiana to help assuage her loneliness. Several of her stories of plantation life appeared in journals. *At Fault*, her first novel, was a story of a St. Louis man who was married to an alcoholic wife, then traveled to Louisiana and fell in love with a Creole widow.

After 1890 Chopin began to sell her stories to such national magazines as *Vogue* and *Century*. Collections of her stories appeared in 1894 (*Bayou Folk*) and 1897 (*A Night in Acadie*) and consisted of sympathetic, humorous tales of Cajuns and Creoles. The exotic background of swamp life, colorful people, and the French Quarter of the Creoles fascinated readers.

The Pontelliers possessed a very charming home on Esplanade Street in New Orleans. It was a large, double cottage, with a broad front veranda, whose round, fluted columns supported the sloping roof. The house was painted a dazzling white; the outside shutters, or jalousies, were green. In the yard, which was kept scrupulously neat, were flowers and plants of every description which flourishes in South Louisiana... The cut glass, the silver, the heavy damask which daily appeared upon the table were the envy of many women whose husbands were less generous than Mr. Pontellier.

The Awakening

Controversial Novel

The definitive novel of Kate Chopin, *The Awakening*, was published in 1899. The story of a married New Orleans woman, Edna Pontellier, opens with her vacationing in nearby Grand Isle, then returning to New Orleans, where she moves out of her husband's house and into a small "pigeon-house." The novel caused a great stir because of Edna's rejection of marriage and traditional values. A prisoner of the society in which she lived, Edna experiences a constant longing for something outside her family and social life and all the inherent responsibilities she wishes to escape.

She could not have told why she was crying. Such experiences as the foregoing were not uncommon in her married life... An indescribable oppression, which seemed to generate in some unfamiliar part of her consciousness, filled her whole being with a vague anguish.

The Awakening

The Awakening was labeled "poison" by one newspaper, and reaction to it was so severe that it adversely affected Kate Chopin's health. Edna Pontellier was happy in her little house and even had several love affairs, but her husband and society were so disapproving that she could not enjoy her secret pleasures.

> In a sweeping passion she seized a glass vase from the table and flung it upon the tiles of the hearth. She wanted to destroy something. The crash and clatter were what she wanted to hear.
>
> *The Awakening*

Although Edna's awakening was tremendous and complete, her joy was tainted with the knowledge that it was not acceptable in her world to be an independent woman.

> The future was a mystery which she never attempted to penetrate. The present alone was significant, was hers, to torture her as it was doing then with the biting conviction that she had lost that which she had held, that she had been denied that which her impassioned, newly awakened being demanded.
>
> *The Awakening*

The Awakening was the final work Kate Chopin published during her lifetime, and it soon went out of print. Although she had moved back to St. Louis and was surrounded by children, friends, and romantic admirers, her health began declining. On August 22, 1904, after spending the day at the St. Louis World Fair, Kate Chopin died from a brain hemorrhage.

During the 1930s, interest was revived in Chopin's works; it then waned again until the 1960s, when Kate Chopin's themes of female independence and her compelling literary style were greatly admired. Today, the works of Kate Chopin continue to grow in popularity.

Josie Arlington—*Storyville Madam*

One of the most famous madams in New Orleans was Josie Arlington, who was born Mary Deubler. Her parents were German, and she was born in New Orleans around 1864. Although she never married, as a young girl Josie became the mistress of one Philip Lobrano, also known as Philip Schwarz. During this nine-year period, Josie Alton (as she called herself) lived in a variety of brothels on Customhouse and Basin Streets.

Miss Alton was known for her cantankerous disposition and her affinity for fighting. In 1886 she lost most of her hair while brawling with a prostitute named Beulah Ripley. Miss Ripley apparently left the scene missing half of an ear and part of her lower lip.

Josie's Brothel

In 1888 Josie opened her own place at 172 Customhouse Street, and it quickly earned a reputation as one of the toughest houses in the city. At this time, she called herself "Josie Lobrano," after her lover, who lived in the house along with a number of Josie's relatives.

On November 2, 1890, Josie and all of her girls were involved in a terrible fight that resulted in her brother, Peter Deubler, being shot by Lobrano. Lobrano was acquitted of the shooting after two trials. Josie broke up with him, changed her name again—this time to Lobrano d'Arlington—and let it be known that her place was thereafter to be filled with gracious women who would only receive refined gentlemen. Josie ran the place with a great deal of success, and after the Storyville district was established in 1897, she opened the Arlington at 225 North Basin Street.

The Arlington

Under Josie's operation, the Arlington soon acquired a reputation of being the grandest of all the bordellos and its illustrious owner, now known as Josie Arlington, as the snobbiest madam in New Orleans. Photos of the Arlington show a four-storied house, complete with bay windows and a cupola on the roof. The interior was gaudily decorated with velvet hangings, chandeliers, Oriental carpets, beveled mirrors, and plenty of gilt.

The Arlington was described in the infamous *Blue Book* (a guide to Storyville's houses and women) as "...absolutely and unquestionably the most decorative and costly fitted out sporting palace ever placed before the American public." With the money she made, Josie Arlington built a $35,000 home on Esplanade Avenue.

Cemetery Monument

In 1905 a fire badly damaged the Arlington, and its notorious owner barely escaped death. While repairs were being made on the house, Josie began to prepare for her demise by purchasing a $2,000 plot in Metairie Cemetery. It was on this plot that she erected the famous reddish marble monument topped with two flambeaux (flaming torches), a cross, and a copper door, at which a young woman knocks, requesting entry.

In her later years, Miss Arlington leased out her brothel and lived in the Esplanade house with her niece, whom she had

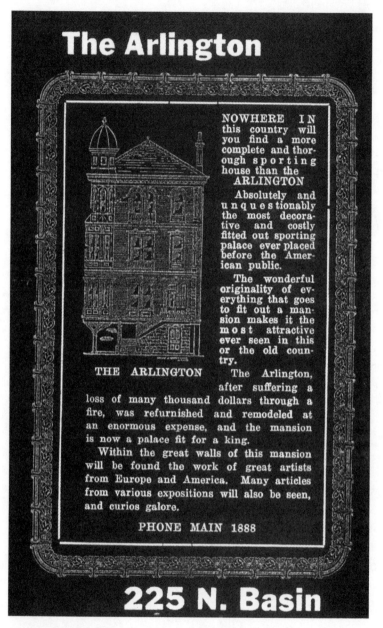

Advertisement of The Arlington, c. 1910. *Historic New Orleans Collection*

educated. She died in her fiftieth year, 1914, and a few months later, the city installed a light that reflected on the tomb, causing a red light to illuminate the madam's final resting place. This spectacle drew so many crowds at night that the light was eventually changed to a white one. Around 1924 Miss Arlington's tomb was sold and her bones placed in a receiving vault.

———

See *Cities of the Dead, Storyville*

New Orleans Remembers

Absinthe—*The Green Fairy*

Absinthe, a fashionable hallucinogenic drink served in New Orleans during the late 1800s and early 1900s, was made of licorice, coriander, aniseed, fennel, and wormwood. Wormwood is a European plant, *Artemisia absinthium*, that yields a bitter dark green oil and is highly addictive. It also gave the drink much of its potency. Wormwood also contains thujone, a chemical much like THC, the active ingredient in marijuana.

With an alcohol content ranging from 60 to 75 percent, absinthe became known for inducing altered states of mind. In 1805 Henri Louis Pernod began manufacturing absinthe in France, and it was soon imported to New Orleans, where it became immensely popular. The factory today still produces an absinthe-like drink. In the latter part of the nineteenth century in Paris, Parisians gathered in cafés to observe *l'heure verte* ("the green hour") and sip absinthe.

The yellow-green liqueur was served using water that dripped into glasses drop by drop, usually over a lump of sugar that made the bitter drink more palatable. The sugar lump rested on a perforated spoon known as an "absinthe spoon." As the sugar and water flowed into the drink, it changed to an

159

opaque yellowish color. Absinthe spoons are highly valued collectors' items.

In 1874 a Spanish bartender named Cayetano Ferrér opened a bar named the "Absinthe House" at 327 Bourbon Street. The establishment soon became a popular gathering place for the more daring members of New Orleans' elite. In the center of the Absinthe House, which was later called the "Old Absinthe House," was a long marble bar that featured a dripping fountain used to serve absinthe. The Old Absinthe House, according to tradition, was where pirate Jean Lafitte and General Andrew Jackson planned the Battle of New Orleans while having absinthe frappés. The drink was often served chilled, particularly on hot summer days.

The "green muse" influenced many artists, including Picasso, Van Gogh, Toulouse-Lautrec, Manet, and Degas, who drank the aperitif at the Absinthe House in New Orleans while visiting relatives and then returned to Paris to paint such masterpieces as *L'Absinthe*. Playwright Oscar Wilde supposedly said of absinthe:

> After the first glass, you see things as you wish they were; after the second, you see things as they are not; finally, you see things as they really are, and that is the most horrible thing in the world.

The drink's negative effects were apparently numerous as well. It was thought to induce absinthism, a syndrome characterized by addiction to absinthe, hyperexcitability, and hallucinations. Absinthe was outlawed by the United States Senate in 1912, after its ban in Switzerland where "absinthe-induced delirium" was blamed for a multiple murder. The New Orleans Absinthe Association managed to keep absinthe dripping, after coming up with a different formula, for twenty-two years. Absinthe made with wormwood is still reportedly available in Spain, Denmark, and Portugal.

Today the Old Absinthe House on Bourbon Street serves a far less potent version of the original drink. Wormwood, absinthe's most potent ingredient, has long been removed. The original Absinthe House, now a bar, is still standing farther down on the famous street and is an excellent example of early nineteenth-century New Orleans architecture. It was built around 1806 and features fanlight transoms on the doors and a wrought-iron balcony railing. The long marble bar, deeply pitted from the many drinks concocted there, is still in place.

The Nuns, the Correction Girls, and the Casket Girls

In 1728 the first of regular arrivals of the so-called *filles à la cassette*, or casket girls, came to Louisiana from France. Developer John Law's Company of the West, known as the Mississippi Company, was attempting to colonize French Louisiana during this time. Early settlers complained about the shortage of suitable mates, so in 1721 the Mississippi Company sent eighty-eight girls, most from a correctional institution, La Salpetriére, in Paris, to the new territory. These women were referred to as the "correction girls" and were cared for by three nuns of the Gray Sisters Order. The correction girls caused a good bit of uproar, and many "could not be restrained," according to Governor Bienville, although at least nineteen were married off shortly after their arrival.

Suitable Wives

The casket girls, on the other hand, were carefully selected from good, middle-class families and were skilled in house-wifely duties. Each young lady was given a small chest (the "casket") containing two shirts, two coats, six headdresses, and other pieces of clothing. Upon their arrival in New Orleans, after a long, arduous journey from France, the casket girls were met by Ursuline nuns, who had come to the settle-ment a few months earlier. The Sisters cared for the girls until husbands could be found for them.

The Old Ursuline Convent

The first group of six Ursuline nuns, also sent to Louisiana under a Mississippi Company contract, arrived in New Orleans in 1727 and founded the Ursuline Convent. They opened a school, began operating a hospital, and cared for orphans. Theirs were the first convent and all girls' school, the Ursuline Academy, in the country.

In 1734 the group moved into a convent, school, and hospital facility located at 301 Chartres Street. Around 1752 the Sisters moved to 1114 Chartres Street, the Old Ursuline Convent, which today houses St. Mary's Church and is one of the oldest brick-and-post structures in the Mississippi Valley. The old building was designed by Ignance François Broutin, Louisiana's Engineer-in-Chief, and features a portico, dormer windows, and pediment. The nuns moved again in 1824 to a building on North Peters Street.

Some of the nuns, most of whom were from middle-class and aristocratic families, brought their knowledge of French cook-ing with them. They also introduced the skills of French embroidery and the making of such fineries as petit point tap-estry. One of the young Sisters, Madeleine Hachard (Sister St.

Stanislaus), kept a diary of her treacherous journey across the seas and gave vivid descriptions of life in the new colony.

Descriptions of Early New Orleans

Madeleine described New Orleans as "...very handsome, well constructed and regularly built, as much as I could judge on the day of our arrival." After that day, she reports, they remained cloistered in their dwelling. The young nun wrote an interesting account of the females already living in New Orleans.

> The women here are extremely ignorant as to the means of securing their salvation, but they are very expert in the art of displaying their beauty. There is so much luxury in this town that there is no distinction among the classes so far as dress goes. The magnificence of display is equal to all.... They paint and rouge to hide the ravages of time, and wear on their faces, as embellishment, small black patches.

She also gave detail of food and living conditions in the colony (see *New Orleans People—Creoles and French*).

The Fate of the Correction Girls

The correction girls were noted by Sister St. Stanislaus as well. Apparently the nuns' attempts to reform them did not go well, and the girls were punished "by putting them upon wooden horses and having them whipped by the regiment of soldiers that guards the town." Eventually, a house of detention was built for the women, and the Ursulines were expected to operate this as well.

The casket girls continued to arrive in the colony until 1751, and many of New Orleans' oldest families proudly trace their lineage to these young girls. It has been said, however, that the casket girls had to have been extraordinarily fertile, having at least one hundred children each, in order to produce as many offspring as have been attributed to them. It may be noted that none of the families claim to be descended from the correction girls.

Storyville

Yes, readers, there really is a house in New Orleans they call The Rising Sun. Located in the French Quarter at 826 S. Louis Street, the structure is also known as "The Dancing Master's House" by those who claim it has never been anything more than a home to prominent citizens. A dancing master sold the home to a widow, Elizabeth Levant, in 1847. "Levant" means "rising" in French, partially explaining the origin of the name.

The tale of Storyville begins with prostitution, which was legal in New Orleans until 1917. "Lewd and Abandoned Women," as they were later referred to in city ordinances, were among the first settlers in the early 1700s. Due to the French influence and a shortage of "respectable" women in the swamp town, these women practiced their trade with few problems until the arrival of the Americans in 1803.

The Americans attempted to regulate the trade by passing laws such as the one prohibiting prostitution on the first floor of any building. In 1857 a law requiring licenses for the girls ($100/year) and their madams ($250/year) was passed, but it was later declared unconstitutional by the courts.

Alderman Story

By 1897 houses of ill repute had sprung up all over the city, to the distress of ordinary citizens, who often didn't appreciate the comings and goings of the bordello next door. After studying red-light districts in Europe, Sidney Story, an alderman and respected businessman, proposed forming a single restricted district in New Orleans that would allow prostitution. The area, on the far side of the French Quarter, was from "the north side of the Customhouse (Iberville) from Lower Basin Street to South Robertson Streets, to the south side of St. Louis from South Robertson to Basin."

Descriptions of Storyville

Although there was a great deal of protest and criticism, an ordinance was passed and upheld by the Louisiana Supreme Court. Soon the ordinary citizens moved out and the "professionals" left the bordellos around town to settle in Storyville, as it became known, to the chagrin of Alderman Story.

Soon cafés, gambling houses, saloons, small bordellos, and opulent Victorian mansions lined the shady streets of Storyville. The better places had stained-glass windows, electric lighting, Oriental rugs, velvet furniture, and fine paintings. Here a gentleman could feast at a sumptuous table, mingle with politicians over brandy, spend the night with a girl of his choosing, and rise the next morning to find his suit and shirt pressed and breakfast ready.

The Notorious *Blue Book* and Other Scandal Sheets

During this period, visitors to New Orleans and regular customers could refer to the notorious *Blue Book*, a red-light district directory, to obtain addresses and descriptions of madams and their houses. The *Blue Book* also contained announcements of new arrivals, many of whom claimed to be "at least 99 44/100 per cent impure."

Other publications, the *Mascot* and the *Sunday Sun*, also served would-be customers. The *Mascot*, established in 1882, was a four- to six-page tabloid issued every Saturday at five cents a copy and contained a gossip column called "Society" that was devoted to the red-light district.

The *Sunday Sun* was known as a "scandal sheet" and usually devoted its headlines to the latest divorce case, murder, or adulterous affair. Its column "Scarlet World" was a frank account of disreputable activities.

The Demise of Storyville

Storyville activities continued unabated until the navy set up camp in New Orleans when America entered World War I in 1917. Josephus Daniels, secretary of the navy, threatened to close down the base unless Storyville was abolished. The district had been in decline for several years, as public sentiment turned against vice and extramarital relations.

On October 9, 1917, the city council adopted an ordinance stating that after midnight of November 12, 1917, it would be unlawful to operate a brothel or assignation house anywhere in New Orleans. There began a mass exodus from the district, as houses were closed and furniture sold to secondhand dealers. Although a few houses continued to operate after the ordinance took effect, they, too, were eventually shut down, and Storyville faded away like the red-gold sun setting on the levee banks. The historic district was razed in the 1930s and replaced with the Iberville Housing project.

———

See *Josie Arlington*

Quadroon Balls

Part of New Orleans' colorful history was the famous Quadroon Balls held during the first half of the 1800s. A "quadroon" legally referred to a person of one-quarter Negro ancestry, but the term was loosely used to describe women of color who were partially white. It was common practice in old New Orleans for white Creole gentlemen to have a quadroon mistress.

An English writer, Harriet Martineau, studied the situation in the 1830s and wrote of the quadroons in her book *Society in America*.

> The quadroon girls of New Orleans are brought up by their mothers to be what they have been; the mistresses of white gentlemen.... The girls are highly educated, externally, and are, probably, as beautiful and accomplished a set of women as can be found. Every young man early selects one, and establishes her in one of those pretty and peculiar houses, whole rows of which may be seen in the Ramparts.

The main purpose of the Quadroon Balls, which took place in lavish ballrooms and theaters, was to introduce the young women to the gentlemen. Both bachelors and married men attended the functions and selected one of the lovely girls to court, usually making the necessary arrangements with the girl's mother. Although the balls were largely ignored by historians and condemned by outsiders, a few New Orleans visitors recorded accounts that spoke of the rare beauty and charm of the girls, some describing them as the most beautiful women ever seen in their travels.

Another English traveler described the girls as "resembling the higher orders of women among the high-class Hindoos; lovely countenances, full, dark, liquid eyes, lips of coral, teeth of pearl, sylph-like figures; their beautifully rounded limbs, exquisite gait, and ease of manner might furnish models for a Venus or Hebe."

One reason married men were so intrigued by the exotic women of color was that many of the marriages in New Orleans during this period were arranged, and once married, the Creole girls devoted themselves to family and home, sometimes leaving husbands bored with the monotony of tradition. Historians are unsure of the origin of the Quadroon Balls. As early as 1786 the quadroons' attire and beauty attracted the attention of Governor Miró, who warned them that their idleness "resulting from their dependence for a livelihood on incontinence and libertinism" would not be tolerated. The young women were known not only for their fancy dress, as opposed to the drab clothing of the Creole women, but also for the plumes on their headdress and the jewelry they wore.

Once the Spanish left and Americans took over the city in 1803, the quadroon women blossomed in New Orleans and in their little white houses along Rampart Street. A quadroon girl's primary goal in life was often to attract a rich white man and become his mistress. Many of the quadroons became life-long partners with their white lovers, bore their children, and lived in relative wealth and ease.

From the 1830s until the 1850s, the Quadroon Balls ruled as some of the most fashionable rendezvous in the city and were spoken of throughout the country. There were two or three balls given per week, and prices were often double those charged at masquerades and white balls. Only white men were admitted for the functions, and efforts were made to limit the guests to gentlemen of means.

By the 1850s the Americanization of New Orleans had set in, and the city in general had outgrown the extravaganzas. The Civil War, which began in 1861, marked the end of the balls, and many quadroons found themselves alone once their men left to defend the Confederacy. Some whose men did not return from the war married men of their own race or moved to northern states, and others remained in their little white houses on Rampart Street.

The Summer of 1853—*Bronze John Pays a Deadly Visit*

From the time yellow fever first invaded New Orleans in the late 1700s, until it was conquered in 1906, New Orleans was known around the world as a "plague spot," according to one writer. Thirty-nine epidemics were recorded in the city between 1796 and 1906.

In 1804 Governor William C.C. Claiborne lost his wife, daughter, and private secretary to yellow fever. The governor, who was in contact with President Thomas Jefferson during this period, kept the concerned president abreast of the horrible situation. Jefferson, who had overseen the purchase of the Louisiana Territory, was very worried that the plague threatened the future of New Orleans and wrote that there was "no spot where yellow fever is so much to be apprehended."

Unhealthy Conditions

Jefferson's fears that the commercial port was doomed did not materialize; in spite of the increasing number of epidemics in the city, ships, immigrants, and fortune-seekers continued to pour into New Orleans. Governor Claiborne also lost his second wife to yellow fever five years later. Reporting her death to President James Madison, Claiborne said the unhealthy condition and location of the governor's mansion were responsible for his wife's death. The governor wrote, "The filth and various matter for putrefaction which accumulate near the water's edge have often proved offensive to me, even when in my chamber."

Yellow fever, which is spread by mosquitoes, found a haven in the city below sea level. The entire city served as a breeding ground for the insects because of the stagnant mud in the streets and general dirtiness of the city. It didn't help that there were also swamps within the city limits.

During the early 1800s New Orleans' sewerage "system" was merely a series of overflowing gutters between the streets and banquettes (sidewalks). Although citizens frequently complained about the gutters and newspapers published stories describing the dreadful conditions of city streets, it was not until 1880, when the city had a population of over 200,000, that the first underground sewer was constructed. It was from the St. Charles Hotel to the Mississippi River.

New Orleans citizens came to fear the dreaded yellow fever epidemics that took place every few years and claimed thousands of lives. The worst scourge occurred in 1853.

The Prosperous Winter of 1852-53

The winter of 1852-53 had brought more than the usual number of ships to town, throngs of people, and the staging of many masked balls. As the weather turned balmy and a bumper cotton crop increased general prosperity, thousands of Irish and German immigrants arrived in the city, providing much-needed labor for the booming town. Some city physicians voiced their usual complaints about unsanitary conditions. May came, the weather got hotter, and the well-to-do families began preparations for their annual summer exodus.

An editor of one newspaper, the *Bee*, wrote in spring of 1853 about New Orleans having "a future so glorious, that imagination can scarcely conceive a more brilliant destiny." Another optimistic editor wrote that since five years had passed without a yellow fever epidemic, the disease itself was "an obsolete idea."

Arrival of Bronze John

May also brought the arrival of ships from Rio de Janeiro and Ireland, and it was reported that there had been sickness on board the ships and even a few burials. A rumor went around that "Bronze John has come to pay a call," but mostly the stories were dismissed. Presumably, the disease was referred to as "Bronze John" due to the yellowish color of its unfortunate victims.

As usual, mosquitoes were causing problems, and citizens slept under "mosquito bars," which consisted of gauze or netting pulled over the bed. Lawyers had huge mosquito frames in their offices that were large enough to cover tables and chairs and allow them to work beneath the netting. Even homemakers often worked with sacks of muslin over their heads and arms to fend off the annoying, biting creatures.

As May ended and June began, more cases of the illness were seen. Doctors sometimes falsified reports of yellow fever in order to prevent panic. Summer rains started, increasing pools of stagnant water and worsening the deplorable street conditions. Human waste, garbage, and mud filled the trenches, providing ripe breeding conditions for mosquitoes.

On July 2 Dr. Abner Hester, a former secretary to the Board of Health, announced that 25 people had died of yellow fever the previous week. The following week, 59 deaths were attributed to Yellow Jack or Saffron Scourge, as the disease was also known. During the week that ended July 16, 204 deaths were reported. Amazingly, many residents remained unconcerned for their safety, since it was commonly believed that only newcomers fell prey to the sickness and that native New Orleanians, Creoles, and Negroes were immune to yellow fever. By July's end, however, deaths from the illness were averaging almost one hundred per day.

Mass Exodus

People began to leave the city in mass numbers, including many city council members. Up the river and at various nearby ports, "shotgun quarantines" were set up, and New Orleans passengers were refused entry. The city council, before adjourning for the summer, had allocated $10,000 to the Board of Health to combat the disease.

Meanwhile, a pall of sickness and death hung over the entire city. "Effluvia," an offensive exhalation or smell, spread the general sickening atmosphere and was believed to be responsible for spreading the fever. In efforts to dispel the stench and halt the epidemic, barrels of tar were kept burning along the levee, and cannons were fired throughout the day and night.

Economic activity was practically at a standstill, and most of the general flurry came as hearse wagons headed from stricken houses to the cemeteries. Gravediggers were much in demand, and unburied bodies began accumulating in the graveyards.

Onset of Yellow Fever

Yellow fever usually struck a person with a mild chill and headache, followed by a temperature. Soon the patient suffered from high fever, delirium, jaundice, and the feared black vomit, which consisted of partially digested blood.

Treatment of the disease often involved the administration of large doses of quinine. There was great debate between the French doctors, who treated the disease with "gentle evacuants, acid drinks with cream of tartar, orange and lemon juice," and the American doctors, who insisted on drastic measures such as dousing the patient with buckets of cold water, bloodletting, and administering mercury in the form of calomel (mercurous chloride).

Horror Stories

Appalling stories of deaths of entire families and pathetic graveyard scenes spread across the country through the newspapers. During one week in August, 1,526 New Orleans citizens died. The entire city smelled of smoke from the tar barrels, burnt gunpowder from cannons, and death. When 269 burials were reported on August 20, one newspaper, the *Delta*, proclaimed the date as "The Black Day."

Other tales of horror abounded. A husband and wife were found dead in their bed, an infant still nursing at his mother's yellowed breast. A second child lay dead on the floor, along with the household servant. A boy and his sister followed workers carrying a coffin containing their father's body, crying, "Pauvre pére, pauvre pére." The two children were apparently the only surviving members of a large French immigrant family.

At hospitals, dying women gave birth, while others, having lost all their children, begged God to take them, too. The sick were laid out on pallets on the grounds, left to beg for water or cry out in delirium as they died.

Stories were told of great generosity as well. Prostitutes became nurses, and nuns, doctors, and priests remained unwavering in their care of the afflicted. One wealthy family was said to have cared for thirty other families. Across the country, charitable citizens sent gifts of money and food to the stricken city.

As sometimes happens in the darkest of times, unusual gaiety was reported. Men toasted departing corpses and bet on the number who would succumb the next day. The body count grew so quickly that it was impossible to bury all the dead, and many were burned or thrown into the Mississippi River.

A few physicians and pharmacists apparently saw the epidemic as a way to make money. Complaints were lodged during the 1853 scourge that the druggists were charging exorbitant prices for medicine and that both doctors and pharmacists conspired to prescribe expensive cures and then shared in the profits. Coffin and ice dealers were also accused of engaging in price gouging.

Relief in September

By the middle of September, the heat and rains lessened. The fever epidemic slowed, and mosquitoes disappeared as the weather changed. People began returning to New Orleans. Restaurants opened, and newcomers once again came to the famous port. Money was collected for orphanages and convalescent homes. Many volunteer organizations were established to help survivors.

Although epidemics continued every few years until 1905, the epidemic of 1853 was by far the worst in the history of New Orleans. Estimates of the number of sick vary, but there were between 30,000 and 40,000 cases of the disease, with approximately 10,000 deaths. Some estimate as many as 15,000 died of the disease.

Immigrants continued to be the most susceptible group to yellow fever. During the Civil War years, when New Orleans was occupied by Union troops, a sanitation program was implemented that seemed to halt the disease. In the latter years of the 1800s, improved drainage and standards of living brought some relief from the dreaded scourge.

In 1900 Walter Reed announced that the disease was transmitted by the *Aedis aegypti* mosquito. This news led the New Orleans Board of Health to begin a mosquito control program, urging citizens to make use of mosquito netting and eliminate deadly breeding grounds.

The final yellow fever outbreak in 1905, with 3,402 cases and 452 deaths reported, resulted in an ambitious mosquito eradication program. With the aid of volunteers, every house and lot in the city were checked for breeding grounds.

> *Whilst waiting to get my baggage, I could smell the offensive effluvium that filled the atmosphere for miles around, resembling that which arises from putrefying animal or vegetable matter.*
>
> Rev. Theodore Clapp
> Unitarian Church
> Arriving in New Orleans after an absence

The Sports Page
From Sugar Bowls to Superdomes and Super Bowls

New Orleans has always been a sports-loving town and has hosted a variety of sporting events from horse races, boxing, and sailing, to more conventional sports like basketball, baseball, and football. Every year, either on New Year's Eve or New Year's Day, the city hosts the Sugar Bowl. New Orleans has also been the site of two heavyweight championship fights.

Tulane University, whose football history dates from 1893, provides the city with an excellent tradition of collegiate football. Tulane and Louisiana State University in Baton Rouge are huge rivals, and their annual game is always a sellout. New Orleans is also a popular spot for Super Bowls, especially since the Superdome is located near the French Quarter. More Super Bowl games have been played in New Orleans than in any other city. Since sports and good times go together, New Orleans is a natural for both.

The New Orleans Pelicans

The New Orleans Pelicans, a minor league team in the Southern Association, existed in New Orleans from 1887 through 1959, winning the pennant during their first year and twelve in subsequent years. Charles Abner Powell was known as the "Father" of the Pelicans, joining the team at its inception in 1887. As manager of the team, Powell invented the rain check, came up with the idea to cover the diamond with tarpaulin during rainstorms to prevent flooding, and introduced the idea of Ladies' Day.

After Powell, other managers included Charley Frank (three pennants), Johnny Dobbs (two pennants), and Larry Gilbert (five pennants). The Pelicans had many players who went on to play in the majors, including Joe Martina, John Oulliber, Eddie Morgan, and Carl Line. The team was disbanded in 1959.

The New Orleans Saints

The National Football League franchise was awarded to New Orleans on November 1 (All Saints' Day), 1966. John Mecom Jr. was the majority stockholder and president of the club, and Vic Schwenk was appointed director of player personnel.

Kicker and former Ole Miss player Paige Cothren was the first player signed, and 42 players were selected in the NFL expansion draft. Training camp began in July in San Diego. The Saints' first preseason game was played August 2, 1967, against Los Angeles in Anaheim, with the Saints losing, 16-7. The team finished the preseason games 5-1, the best preseason record ever for a first-year expansion team. The first regular season game was also a loss to Los Angeles, 27-13, on September 17. The Saints won their first regular NFL game on November 5, 1967, in a 31-24 victory over Philadelphia at Tulane Stadium.

Vic Schwenk replaced Bert Rose as general manager in 1968, and wide receiver Dave Parks signed up to play. The team wound up with a 4-9-1 record and third-place finish in Century Division. Defensive tackle Dave Rowe went on to play in the Pro Bowl.

In 1969 Tom Dempsey kicked a 55-yard field goal against the Los Angeles Rams, the longest field goal kicked in the NFL that season and one foot short of the pro football record. The team emerged with a 5-9 record, continuing to hold the NFL expansion team record with a three-year report of 12-29-1.

In 1970 J.D. Roberts replaced Tom Fears as head coach, and the Saints, along with San Francisco, Los Angeles, and Atlanta, formed the Western Division of the National Conference. On November 8, Tom Dempsey kicked the longest field goal in NFL history—63 yards against Detroit.

Quarterback Archie Manning was drafted in 1971, and quarterback Bill Kilmer was traded to Washington for linebacker Tom Roussel, plus 4th and 8th round picks in the 1972 draft. On August 11 construction of the Louisiana Superdome was begun. The Saints defeated the Cowboys 24-20 in New Orleans on October 17, and the Cowboys went on to win the Super Bowl.

In 1972 Richard F. Gordon Jr. was appointed executive vice president of the Saints. John North became the team's third head coach in 1973, replacing J. D. Roberts. The Saints finished the season 5-9. In 1974 the Saints once again finished their season 5-9, tying the best mark in their history.

The Louisiana Superdome was dedicated on August 3, 1975, and on August 9 the first game was played in the structure, the Saints losing 13-7 against Houston. Ernie Hefferie, director of pro personnel, replaced John North as head coach on an interim basis.

In 1976 the Saints hired Hank Stram as their fourth head coach. Chuck Muncie won the team's season rushing and touchdown records in 1977. Hank Stram was replaced by Dick Nolan as head coach in 1978. The same year, Archie Manning won the Byron White Award for contributions to his team, community, and country. The Saints had their first win at Los Angeles Coliseum on October 22, when they upset the Rams 10-3. They also beat the 49ers 24-13 at the Superdome on December 3, 1978. The season ended as their best with a 7-9 record. Archie Manning was named Player of the Year and MVP in the National Conference and was selected to play in the Pro Bowl.

The 1979 season ended 8-8, setting another team record, and Steve Rosenbloom was brought in as executive vice president and general manager. In 1980 the Saints were represented in the Pro Bowl by Chuck Muncie, who was selected MVP, Archie Manning, Tommy Myers, Wes Chandler, and Henry Childs. Their regular season was marked by a 14-game losing streak, which finally ended December 14 with a 21-20 win over the Jets in a snowstorm at Shea Stadium.

Steve Rosenbloom, along with vice president of player personnel Dick Steinberg, resigned in 1981, and O.A. (Bum) Phillips became head coach. In the NFL draft, the Saints selected running back and 1980 Heisman Trophy winner George Rogers as their first overall choice. Rogers became the 1981 NFL rushing champion and all-time NFL rookie rusher with 1,674 yards for the season.

In 1982 Eddie Jones became the president of the Saints, and O.A. (Bum) Phillips was named general manager in addition to his coaching title. Archie Manning was traded to the Houston Oilers for tackle Leon Gray. The Saints defense was ranked as No. 1 in the NFL. The NFL Players Association went on strike in September, and games did not resume until November 21, when the Saints defeated Kansas City 27-17 in the Superdome. On December 19 halfback George Rogers gained 166 yards rushing at Dallas, setting the top individual performance in the NFL and the Saints' single-game record.

In 1983 halfback George Rogers set the team's single-game record by rushing for 206 yards in a 28-17 win over St. Louis at the Superdome. The Saints finished the season 8-8, narrowly missing the playoffs, but with the NFL's No. 1 defense overall and the No. 1 defense against the pass.

Linebacker Rickey Jackson went to the Pro Bowl in Honolulu in 1984. The Saints acquired veteran quarterback Richard Todd from the New York Jets and running back Earl Campbell from Houston. On November 19 the club had their first win on prime time television with a 27-24 victory over the Pittsburgh Steelers in the Superdome. On November 26 owner John Mecom Jr. announced that the team was for sale.

The Saints were represented in the 1985 Pro Bowl by linebacker Rickey Jackson, defensive end Bruce Clark, and punter Brian Hansen. Tom Benson negotiated with Mecom for purchase of the franchise and became the new owner on May 31, 1985. Head Coach Bum Phillips resigned in November, and Defensive Coordinator Wade Phillips was named interim head coach.

In 1986 Jim Finks was named president and general manager and also became part owner. Wade Phillips was released, and Jim Mora was named head coach. Scouting was restructured, and new uniforms were designed, featuring the fleur-de-lis logo inside the state of Louisiana on the jersey and pants. A training camp was opened in Hammond, Louisiana, at Southeastern Louisiana University. The team finished the season 7-9.

In 1987 construction began on improvements to the Superdome. On September 21 the NFL Players Association announced that a strike would begin the following Monday.

The Saints' games resumed October 4, when they defeated the Rams 37-10 in the Superdome. On October 25, 1987, following the Saints' defeat 24-22 to the 49ers, Coach Jim Mora made his famous "coulda, woulda, shoulda" speech to the media. The team finished the season with a 12-3 record.

The Saints hosted the wild card game against the Vikings, who won 44-10. Six Saints—K Morten Andersen, TE Hoby Brenner, G Brad Edelman, RB Rueben Mayes, LB Sam Mills, and CB Dave Waymer—were picked for the AFC-NFC Pro Bowl. President and General Manager Jim Finks was honored as the NFL executive of the year, and Head Coach Jim Mora was named NFL coach of the year. Mora signed a five-year contract with the team. On July 16 the players reported to a new training camp at the University of Wisconsin-La Crosse. The team scored their biggest win ever on November 20 against Denver, 41-0. The win marked the Saints' second consecutive winning season.

The Saints were represented in the 1989 Pro Bowl by K Morten Anderson, LB Sam Mills, and WR Eric Martin. During June 2-4 the Who Dat! Fan Club hosted its first convention at the Hyatt. The club, which had its origins from a cheer shouted at games, boasted 12,000 fans, and the convention was attended by 1,000 people. The team finished the 1989 season with a 9-7 record.

Chosen to appear in the Pro Bowl from 1989's roster were RB Dalton Hilliard, LB Vaughan Johnson, and LB Pat Swilling. The Saints participated in American Bowl '90 in London August 5, 1990, winning against the Raiders 17-10 in Wembley Stadium. In the NFL draft, the team traded Nos. 1 and 3 draft choices in 1991 and conditional No. 2 draft choice to Dallas for quarterback Steve Walsh. The Saints finished the season 8-8.

In a wild card game, the Bears defeated the Saints 16-6 January 6, 1991, at Soldier Field. It was the team's second playoff game in their history. On December 22 the Saints beat the Cardinals 27-3 in Phoenix and won their first NFC West title. The Falcons defeated New Orleans in a 27-20 playoff game in the Superdome December 28.

Linebackers Vaughan Johnson, Sam Mills, and Pat Swilling were chosen for the Pro Bowl. The 1992 schedule contained four prime-time games, the most in team history. President/General Manager Jim Finks and Head Coach Jim Mora signed new three-year contracts. The Saints made the playoffs for the third consecutive year and won the NFC wild card game 20-0 over the New York Jets in the Meadowlands. On January 3, 1993, the Philadelphia Eagles defeated the Saints in a second wild card game, 36-20 at the Superdome. The 1992 season finished with the Saints leading in points allowed, 202, a team record. Six Saints—linebackers Rickey Jackson, Vaughan Johnson, Sam Mills, and Pat Swilling, kicker Morten Anderson, and center Joel Hilgenberg were chosen for the Pro Bowl.

In April of 1993 the Saints acquired quarterback Wade Wilson from Atlanta. President and General Manager Jim Finks was diagnosed with cancer in the same month. A bill calling for Superdome renovations and a new practice facility passed state lawmakers in Baton Rouge.

Finks resigned in July for health reasons. On December 26 rookie Tyrone Hughes returned a punt 83 yards for a touchdown, the longest in team history, in a 37-26 loss to the Eagles in Philadelphia. Three Saints, linebackers Renaldo Turnbill and Rickey Jackson and punk/kick returner Tyrone Hughes, were chosen to represent the team in the Pro Bowl. The team closed the season with a 20-13 victory over the Cincinnati Bengals, leaving them with an 8-8 record.

In January of 1994 Jim Miller was promoted to executive vice president of administration. The club acquired quarterback Jim Everett from the Los Angeles Rams. Jim Finks died May 8 after battling lung cancer. The team signed a five-year contract with the training camp in La Crosse, Wisconsin. Winning their season finale 30-28 over Denver at Mile High Stadium, the Saints finished the regular season 7-9, their first losing record since 1986. Tackle William Roaf and cornerback Eric Allen represented the Saints at the Pro Bowl.

On January 19, 1996, Bill Kuharich was named vice president and general manager. The team moved to a new facility in Metairie on April 15, and, for the first time in their history, the entire organization was housed under one roof. After a defeat 19-7 by the Carolina Panthers, Head Coach Jim Mora resigned, ending a 10 ½-year tenure with the team. Rick Venturi was named interim head coach. The team saw a string of seven losses until December 15, when they beat the New York Giants 17-3.

In 1997 Bill Kuharich was named president/general manager/chief operating officer of the Saints, and he named former Chicago Bears coach Mike Ditka the new head coach of the team.

The Saints ended the 1997 season with six wins and ten losses. Their touchdown catch leader was WR Andre Hastings, who recently signed a three-year contract.

In 1998 the New Orleans Saints signed unrestricted free agent cornerback Tyronne Drakeford and linebacker Kevin Mitchell away from NFC West rival San Francisco, after losing LB Winfred Tubbs and TE Irv Smith to the 49ers. The team also lost linebacker Ernest Dixon to the Carolina Panthers. Safety Chad Cota left the Panthers to head for a three-year stint with the Saints.

For the 1998 season, Head Coach Mike Ditka plans to "evaluate personnel and try to go back and look at everything we've done. Try to see if we can come to some kind of agreement as a staff in understanding if we believe everything we're doing is the right thing or if we should change things based on our personnel." One thing is definite, though, and that is that New Orleanians are one hundred percent behind their team!

New Orleans History

Early Exploration and Settlement

The city of New Orleans has been likened to a giant bowl. Situated as it is on the bank of the Mississippi River and actually below sea level, one must wonder why anybody wanted to build a city in a place where floods were common, epidemics rampant, and summer heat intolerable.

Although Native Americans had lived in the vicinity for a long time, French explorer René-Robert Cavalier de la Salle came to a site approximately forty miles below New Orleans in 1682 and claimed the whole area for French King Louis XIV. La Salle named the area "Louisiana" in honor of the king and his wife, Austrian-born Queen Anne.

Other explorers soon followed, most notably Sieur de Bienville and Sieur d'Iberville. With the aid of Choctaw Indians, the two explorers found a place at the mouth of the Mississippi River in 1699, which they named "Pointe du Mardi Gras." One of the primary purposes of their voyage was to find an easy route into the Mississippi and thereby control trade in the area.

Along a crescent curve of the river was a site that was the shortest route to the Gulf of Mexico and seemed relatively well drained. It was also a good place to establish a fort and assume control of the lower Mississippi. In 1718 Bienville established New Orleans as the capital of Louisiana.

John Law and the Company of the West

In the meantime, John Law, a Scottish businessman, had created a development company in 1716 to colonize the area. The Company of the West, as it was known, took money from investors in exchange for land in Louisiana.

With the help of convicts and carpenters, Bienville laid out the city and even built a three-foot artificial levee. Eventually, a grid pattern of streets was drawn up to replace the random scattering of huts that blew over during a hurricane. Help came from engineers Pierre Blond de la Tour and Adrien de Pauger.

> *It is very disagreeable for an officer charged with the defense of a colony to have . . . only a band of deserters, smugglers and scoundrels, who are all ready not only to abandon you but also to turn against you.*
>
> Governor Bienville, 1719

The little settlement lacked many things, but most notably, it was lacking in settlers. Law had pledged to investors that there would be 6,000 settlers and 3,000 slaves in the colony by 1727. Bienville was selected as the first governor of the colony, and he persuaded a group of Ursuline nuns to come over. The nuns operated a school, hospital, and a home for orphans. The famous "casket girls" or *filles à la cassette* came during this period (1728-1751) also. Along with the casket

girls, there were large groups of male and female convicts
sent to populate the new colony.

Early Struggles

The little settlement struggled with crime, floods, Indian
attacks, and epidemics, but it continued to grow as new ship-
ments of colonists and supplies arrived regularly. Its prime
location on the river was very much conducive to growth, and
the abundance of game and seafood made life a little easier
for the new settlers.

John Law continued to promote Louisiana as a paradise
abundant with treasures. Needless to say, newcomers were
frequently disappointed upon their arrival but were soon
comforted by not only the survival skills of the French, but
their culinary capability as well.

Law's advertisements brought an influx of Germans in the
1720s. Although many died en route to Louisiana, those
who settled the region were stable and hardworking. A
large group of slaves arrived in 1720, and a census in 1721
recorded 470 men, women, and children, including 172
slaves. Sixteen hundred Acadians who had been driven out
of France and then Canada came to New Orleans during the
French reign and continued to arrive for a number of years.
These persecuted people were soon to make themselves at
home in the swamps and backwoods of Louisiana. Their
descendants are today referred to as "Cajuns."

Although the Indians were usually friendly and helpful to the
French, several battles—in 1736, 1739, and 1740—pitted the
two groups against each other. In 1743 a discouraged and
tired Bienville resigned his position.

Spanish Rule

The Treaty of Fontainebleu transferred New Orleans and the vast Louisiana Territory to the Spanish in 1762. Since the treaty took place in secret, Louisiana citizens didn't learn of the transfer for months. New Orleans citizens were very unhappy with the prospect of rule by the Spanish, and when Spanish Governor Don Antonio de Ulloa arrived, he was chased away to Havana by a group of colonists. The King of Spain sent General Don Alexander "Bloody" O'Reilly (an Irishman in the king's army) and 2,600 men to restore order to the city. Many of the rebels were executed by firing squad.

The Spanish brought with them a new, more orderly way of doing things. They built the Cabildo to house the government, as well as many other buildings, some of which were destroyed by various fires. Nevertheless, Spanish architecture abounds in the French Quarter. The Spaniards also influenced culinary practices and introduced such traditional Spanish dishes as paella.

Transfer of Louisiana

Spain continued to rule Louisiana until 1800, when it was transferred back to the French in the Treaty of San Ildefonso. Almost before the residents of New Orleans found out the French had regained control of their city (this treaty was also secured in secret), the Americans bought the Louisiana Territory in 1803 for fifteen million dollars.

The thought of being governed by the "Wild Kaintucks," as American frontiersmen were known, put fear into the hearts of the French and Spanish residents. A group of Ursuline nuns were so upset, they went to Cuba (the sisters eventually returned). The Louisiana Territory was formally transferred from Spain to France on November 30, 1803, in the Cabildo, and then to the United States on December 20.

American Rule

The Americans brought grandeur and great wealth into New Orleans—of course, the Creoles thought the Yankees were garish and unrefined. Soon, New Orleans was the largest city in the South and a great worldwide shipping port.

The Battle of New Orleans

In 1812 Louisiana became a state, and also in the same year, the United States went to war against Great Britain. By 1814 there were rumors that the British were heading to attack New Orleans.

General Andrew Jackson was in New Orleans in 1814 and, although he was ill, managed to enlist Indians, free people of color, and many New Orleans citizens to help him fight the British. Even pirate Jean Lafitte helped with supplies and men. The battle took place six miles from the French Quarter, on the banks of the Mississippi River at a settlement called Chalmette.

It was late December 1814 and bitter cold when Jackson first attacked the British as they were camped along the river. The British forces were being led by General Edward Pakenham, who had recently defeated Napoleon. The attacks continued through the new year, as the British fought back with rein-forcements who were being sent to their aid.

Finally, on January 8, 1815, came the decisive battle. Americans were fighting behind mud ramparts and bales of cotton. General Pakenham was mortally wounded, and one of his officers later referred to Jackson's troops as "the most murderous and destructive fire of all arms ever poured upon a column."

When it was all over, the Americans suffered seven killed and six wounded. The British lost over 300 men, with another 2,000 wounded or missing. After ten days, they left the area. Although the Battle of New Orleans was fought two weeks after the Treaty of Ghent that ended the war was signed, it marked the last time blood was shed between the two countries, and its decisive victory sent Andrew Jackson to the White House.

Growth of New Orleans

Following the War of 1812, English-speaking Americans arrived in great numbers and were so despised by the native Creoles that a "neutral ground" was designated to divide the French and American communities. That same neutral ground today is Canal Street.

The cotton and sugar trades were thriving, and the port city of New Orleans grew not only in numbers but in sophistication and culture as well. In spite of floods, cholera, and yellow fever, people continued to immigrate to New Orleans, particularly the Irish, German, and French. Mosquitoes, which spread yellow fever (although this wasn't known until 1900), were so bad that people often worked and slept under mosquito netting.

The Civil War

The city was very lively and noisy this evening with rockets and lights in honor of secession.... We hastened home to dress for a soirée, but on the stairs Edith said, "G., first come and help me dress Phoebe and Chloe [the negro servants]. There is a ball to-night in aristocratic colored society. This is Chloe's first introduction to New Orleans circles, and Henry Judson, Phoebe's husband, gave five dollars for a ticket for her." Chloe is a recent purchase from Georgia. We superintended their very stylish toilets, and Edith said, "G., run into your room, please, and write a pass for Henry. Put Mr. D.'s name on it."
"Why, Henry is free," I said.—"That makes no difference; all colored people must have a pass if out late."

War Diary of a Union Woman in the South
1861

By 1860 New Orleans was one of the wealthiest cities in the nation and had the world's largest cotton market. It was also the world's greatest export center. Unfortunately, the city's good fortune was interrupted on February 4, 1861, when Louisiana seceded from the Union. Many New Orleans citizens opposed the decision, but they didn't have much choice in the matter.

The Mississippi River was blockaded by Union ships in May of 1861, cutting New Orleans off from many imports. Because the river was so vital to survival, the Union continued their attempts to seize all fortifications along the

Mississippi. A fierce battle took place in the Gulf of Mexico near Ship Island.

In New Orleans, panic ensued as warehouses of cotton, food, and lumber were burned to keep them from enemy hands. On May 1, 1862, Major General Benjamin "Spoons" Butler and his Union soldiers took control of the city, because Union Captain David Farragut's fleet was able to pass through the Confederate forts.

New Orleans surrendered to Union forces without a single shot being fired. The Union occupied New Orleans throughout the war and for some twelve years afterward—the longest occupation of any Southern city. Butler's reign in New Orleans was tempestuous, and he was loathed by the citizens. Anyone not pledging loyalty to the Union was subject to having their possessions seized, and Butler was alleged to have been partial to seizing sterling flatware—hence, the nickname "Spoons."

Union soldiers were so hated that ladies insulted them and tossed slop jars on their heads, prompting Butler to issue his famous Order 28, which said that "...any women (calling themselves ladies) who by word, gesture or movement, insults or shows contempt for any officer of the United States, shall be regarded as a woman of the town plying her avocation."

Reconstruction

It was said by one writer that shooting didn't start in New Orleans until after the war. The so-called Reconstruction period following the war was marked by chaos and terrible rioting. Emancipated slaves were set free with no place to go, and many from surrounding plantations converged on New Orleans.

Even though Louisiana was readmitted to the Union in 1868, anti-Union sentiment ran high, particularly in light of continued Union occupation of the city. On January 18, 1873, two governors were inaugurated—William Pitt Kellogg, Republican, and John McEnery, Democrat. The Republican ceremonies were held in the Mechanics' Institute in New Orleans, and the Democrats held theirs in Lafayette Square. Kellogg's rule prevailed for four years, due to the support of President Ulysses S. Grant, but Kellogg's effectiveness was decreased in 1874 when a French Quarter riot involving ten thousand men took place. The Battle of Liberty, as it was known, was a showdown between the carpetbag government and a group known as the White League.

Return to Normalcy

Although controversy and chaos continued in Louisiana and its government for several more years, trade and commerce gradually improved until New Orleans was once more a thriving port. Immigration continued to bring diversity to the city's rich cultural life. Toward the end of the nineteenth century, Italians were the largest group of immigrants.

With the turn of the century and the discovery of yellow fever's source, the city was able to soon eradicate the yellow fever problem. The new century brought plenty of other changes as well. The French Quarter fell into decay as a new downtown with skyscrapers began to develop.

Sugarcane, oil, shipping, and lumber were the state's primary industries. New Orleans was still a party town, however, and a 1900 census reported approximately 2,000 bars in the city. The horse and buggy were the primary form of transportation, and a raucous new form of snazzy music called "jazz" was being played on the street corners.

Even though many of the Reconstruction battles were over, New Orleans would not regain its pre-Civil War status as the second wealthiest city in the United States. President Theodore Roosevelt visited the city in 1905, which gave New Orleans back some of its old self-confidence. During the 1920s, a preservation group organized to save French Quarter buildings from demolition and to begin restoring them to their past elegance.

Political Machine

Politically, there was still turmoil in New Orleans. Martin Behrman, a politician from Algiers, was elected mayor five times in the first quarter of the century, dying in office in 1926. A political machine, known as the Regular Democratic Organization, developed and enforced its rule through jobs at City Hall. Those hired were expected to follow the machine's rules and candidates. The Industrial Canal, which provided location for industries, was built under Behrman's rule.

The "Old Regular" machine became known as the New Orleans Ring, and its candidates stayed in power until the late '20s and early '30s, when Huey Long, a politician from north Louisiana, came to power as state senator and governor.

A bitter enemy of the Ring, Long's influence was felt throughout New Orleans politics. Long was able to break the machine and get control of the city by passing legislation that gave the state power over police and fire departments and even taxation policies. Long's politics almost drove New Orleans into bankruptcy. He was assassinated in 1935.

President Franklin D. Roosevelt visited New Orleans in 1937, an event which became known as the Second Louisiana

Purchase, because it healed some of the estrangement that had come about between Louisiana and the national government during the Huey Long years.

World War II and Beyond

World War II brought a great expanse of New Orleans' shipbuilding and port industries, restoring the city to some of its earlier prominence. Postwar New Orleans saw benefits from the oil industry but growth in racial strife when New Orleans public schools were ordered desegregated in 1956. Many whites left the city and headed for the suburbs, taking with them a large share of the tax base that would have gone for city improvement.

Crime and poverty became major problems. The suburbs around New Orleans prospered, while the inner city fell victim to urban blight, homelessness, and decay, with the exception of the business district. During the '70s, '80s, and '90s, tourism became one of New Orleans' biggest industries.

The 1984 World's Fair, while unsuccessful financially, brought about development of riverfront property, including the Riverwalk, a collection of shops and restaurants along the levee.

The restoration of the French Quarter and an international interest in jazz and Creole and Cajun cooking, as well as Mardi Gras, all bring millions of visitors to the city. Riverboat gambling has also contributed to the ongoing popularity of New Orleans as a vacation spot.

As New Orleans enters the twenty-first century, it faces the same problems as any other major United States city—lack of funds for city improvement, crime, etc. But New Orleans' laissez-faire attitude guarantees that no matter what happens in the rest of the country, in New Orleans, the good times will keep rolling.

———

See *New Orleans People*

New Orleans No-Nos

Things You Should Never Do in New Orleans

1.   Do not go into St. Louis No. 1 Cemetery on June 23, which is known as "St. John's Eve" in the practice of voodoo. Marie Laveau is believed to be buried in this cemetery, and her followers gather here on St. John's Eve to pay homage to the former voodoo queen.

2.   Never call the city "New Orleens." You will be labeled one of those damned Yankees. It's "N'Yawlins," New Or-lee-unz," or "New Orlunz."

3.   Never get arrested. New Orleans is notorious for holding people in jail, unless they have a friend in local politics who will speak with the judge. It's very difficult to get bonded out quickly in the Crescent City.

4.   Never accept an invitation to a hurricane party, unless you enjoy riding out terrifying winds and storms. (People who give these parties refuse to evacuate when ordered to do so.)

5.   Don't walk down Bourbon Street if you shock easily. This street is definitely rated XXX.

New Orleans Timeline

1682	French explorer LaSalle stops at an Indian village at or near present-day New Orleans and erects a cross several miles above the mouth of the Mississippi River. He names the territory "Louisiana" and claims the area for King Louis XIV.
1699	Explorer brothers Iberville and Bienville enter Mississippi River from the Gulf of Mexico and leave men on shore to build protection for Louisiana.
1717	John Law's Company of the West plans development of Louisiana and orders establishment of New Orleans, named for Duc d'Orléans, Regent of France.
1718	With the assistance of engineers Pauger and Blond de la Tour, Bienville lays out the streets of New Orleans.
1720	First slave shipment arrives in Louisiana.
1722	Capital of Louisiana is moved to New Orleans.
1724	Bienville enacts the *Code Noir* regulating slaves and their owners.

1727	Ursuline nuns arrive and begin a convent school for girls.
1728	Arrival of first "casket girls" from France.
1729	News of an Indian massacre in nearby Natchez prompts construction of ditch and stockade against possible attack.
1743	New Orleans enters an era of high social life under Governor Vaudreuil (1743-1753).
1763	Louis XV gives Louisiana to his cousin, Charles III of Spain; Jesuits are expelled from Louisiana by French authorities.
1764	First Acadians migrate to Louisiana from New York.
1768	Open rebellion against Spanish rule causes Governor Ulloa to flee for Spain.
1769	Arrival of General Alexander O'Reilly and his troops, who take possession of the city and execute six rebellion leaders. Cabildo is established.
1779	Spanish order construction of enclosed market to prevent exposure of food to outdoor air. This market became known as the French Market.
1788	Fires devastate city, destroying over 800 dwellings.
1791	First professional theatrical performances held in the city by Louis Tabary and his company from Santo Domingo.
1794	First newspaper, *Le Moniteur de la Louisiana*, is published. Fire again destroys much of the city;

	Spanish architects supervise much of the rebuilding.
1795	Étienne de Boré perfects sugar refining. Carondelet Canal opens, connecting the city with Bayou St. John.
1803	Nov. 30-Dec. 20 Spain gives Louisiana back to France; French flag flown in Place d'Armes. Dec. 20—United States takes possession of Louisiana Purchase territory; ceremonies in Cabildo.
1815	Andrew Jackson leads Creoles and Americans to victory over invading British in the Battle of New Orleans.
1821	Artist John James Audubon, while living in New Orleans, regularly visits wild bird and game sellers at the French Market to purchase "models" for his paintings.
1837	First issue of the *Picayune* is published.
1847	University of Louisiana, later Tulane University, founded.
1849	Worst steamboat explosion at levee; 86 people killed.
1850	Irish potato famine refugees come to New Orleans.
1853	City's worst yellow fever epidemic kills approximately 10,000 people.
1857	First theme ball and parade presented by Comus.
1860	Of the 168,675 residents of New Orleans, approximately 40 percent were foreign-born,

including around 24,000 Irish and 14,000 German.

1861	Louisiana secedes from United States.
1862	New Orleans falls to Union forces; Union Commander Benjamin Butler, in an effort to eliminate yellow fever, orders cleaning of all New Orleans markets, which were described as "filthy."
1870	Author Kate Chopin arrives in New Orleans.
1872	First King of Carnival, Rex, establishes Mardi Gras as official holiday.
1903	Establishment of large gypsy camp on St. Louis and Scott Streets.
1909	Last yellow fever epidemic.
1921	Mississippi River is connected with Lake Pontchartrain via the Industrial Canal.
1935	First Sugar Bowl played between Tulane (20) and Temple (14).
1957	Federal judge orders desegregation of public schools.
1958	Mississippi River Bridge opens, connecting the east and west banks of New Orleans.
1961	Space Age comes to New Orleans when the National Aeronautics and Space Administration takes over the Michoud assembly factory, employing thousands of people to build rockets.
1966	National Football League awards franchise to John Mecom Jr., and the New Orleans Saints are born.

1969	Clay Shaw, New Orleans businessman, goes on trial for conspiracy in assassination of President John F. Kennedy. Shaw is acquitted.
1977	First black mayor since Reconstruction, Ernest N. "Dutch" Morial, is elected.
1984	World's Fair held in New Orleans.
1986	Jim Mora named head coach of the New Orleans Saints.
1993	Riverboat gambling returns to New Orleans with the opening of riverboat casinos.
1997	Former Chicago Bears coach Mike Ditka named new head coach of the New Orleans Saints; New Orleans hosts Super Bowl for the eighth time.
	Zephyr Stadium opens to host the New Orleans Zephyrs, a AAA baseball team.
1999	Opening of New Orleans Sports Arena, to be used for concerts, basketball, and ice hockey games. Across the street from the Superdome.

New Orleans Notables

Below are listed a few people who made the Crescent City what it is today. Notables whose names are mentioned elsewhere in the book are not included in this list.

Benjamin, Judah P. (1811-1884)—U.S. senator and New Orleans lawyer who served as attorney general, secretary of war, and secretary of state in the Confederate cabinet; called the "brains of the Confederacy"; after the war, he escaped to England, where he continued to practice law.

Caldwell, James H. (1793-1863)—English actor who promoted New Orleans and became a real estate developer; started gas company and became a politician; built the first American theater on Camp Street.

Clark, Daniel (1766-1813)—Irish-American businessman and land owner who aided Thomas Jefferson in the Louisiana Purchase and later wounded Governor Claiborne in a duel.

Delgado, Issac (1839-1912)—wealthy sugar planter who established art gallery, Delgado Museum, which became the New Orleans Museum of Art, and Delgado College, a technical school.

Eads, James B. (1820-1887)—American engineer who designed a jetty system at the mouth of the Mississippi to keep the channel from closing up due to silt.

Gumbel, Bryant—television journalist.

Hearn, Lafcadio (1850-1904)—writer who wrote for the *Item* and *Times-Democrat* and authored acclaimed novel *Chita*, published in 1889, that chronicled the tragedy of a tidal wave striking New Orleans.

Hector, François Louis, Baron de Carondelet (1748-1807)— Belgian nobleman who governed Spanish Louisiana from 1792 to 1797; during his rule, first theater opened, street lights were put up, night watchman was provided, navigation canal was dug, and first newspaper, *Moniteur de la Louisiane*, was printed.

Jackson, Mahalia—internationally renowned gospel singer.

Kenner, Duncan Farrar (1813-1887)—active Confederate who helped rid the state of carpetbaggers following the Civil War.

Lafon, Thomy (1810-1893)—philanthropist and free man of color.

Larroquette, John—actor and 1985 Emmy-winner for role in *Night Court*.

Llula, José (1810?-1888)—an unusually good swordsman who was known for fighting duels throughout his life.

Louis, Jean (1690?-1736)—sailor who bequeathed his money to establish a hospital for the poor that eventually became Charity Hospital.

Marigny, Bernard de (1785-1868)—member of established Creole family; imported crap shooting to New Orleans; compulsive gambler.

Matas, Rudolph (1862-1957)—well-known surgeon who was a pioneer in vascular surgery; one of the first physicians to support theory that yellow fever was transported by a mosquito.

Menken, Adah Issacs (1835-1868)—sensational actress who achieved international fame.

Newcomb, Josephine Louise LeMonnier (1816-1901)—endowed a college for women within Tulane University as a memorial to her daughter, Sophie Newcomb.

Ochsner, Alton (1896-1981)—renowned surgeon and founder of Ochsner Hospital and Oschner Clinic; first to relate cigarette smoking to lung cancer.

Peters, Samuel Jarvis (1801-1855)—early real estate entrepreneur who developed New Orleans above Canal Street; known for development of the "American" sector of the city.

Pinchback, Pinkey Benton Stuart (1837-1921)—black politician who was lieutenant governor during Reconstruction.

Pollock, Oliver (1737-1823)—Irish-American New Orleans merchant; agent for Continental Congress; patriot who helped finance American Revolution.

Poydras, Julien (1740-1824)—philanthropist and poet; established dowry fund for underprivileged maidens.

Rillieux, Norbert (1806-1884)—free person of color who was educated in France; scientific experiments led to evaporation process used in the manufacture of sugar.

Roquette, Adrien Emanuel (1813-1888)—Creole poet and priest; medicine man with the Choctaws; led an ascetic life.

Roquette, François Dominique (1812-1890)—vagabond and troubadour whose eccentricity made him a colorful New Orleans character.

Slidell, John (1793-1871)—prominent in state and national politics during 1850s; Minister to France under the Confederacy.

Soulé, Pierre (1801-1870)—political refugee from France who became a prominent criminal lawyer and politician in New Orleans; champion of states' rights.

Touro, Judah (1775-1854)—New Orleans philanthropist.

Tulane, Paul (1801-1887)—New Orleans philanthropist and founder of Tulane University.

Wright, Sophie Bell (1866-1912)—teacher and humanitarian who established night schools and many social service agencies.

You Haven't Lived Until You've...

Favorite Things Natives Like to Do in New Orleans

...eaten beignets and drank café-au-lait at the Café du Monde.

...ridden the ferry to Algiers and back.

...eaten spicy crawfish at a crawfish boil—the natives like to peel 'em and suck the heads to get all the spice!

...driven through one of many Drive-Through Daiquiri stands and indulged yourself.

...visited "Christmas in the Oaks" in City Park.

...attended the Blessing of the Shrimp Fleet.

...gone fishing in Bucktown, a fishing village inside New Orleans.

...sat on the levee watching ships and barges go by, remembering the original settlers who established the Crescent City.

References

Asbury, Herbert. (1938). *The French Quarter*. Garden City, NY: Garden City Publishing Co., Inc.

Berry, Jason, Foose, Jonathan, & Jones, Tad. (1986). *Up From the Cradle of Jazz: New Orleans Music Since World War II*. Athens, GA: The University of Georgia Press.

Bodin, Ron. (1990). *Voodoo Past and Present*. Lafayette, LA: University of Southwestern Louisiana.

Bultman, Bethany Ewald. (1996). *New Orleans*. Fodor's Travel Publications, Inc. Oakland, CA: Compass American Guides.

Carter, H. (Ed.). (1968). *The Past as Prelude: New Orleans 1718-1968*. New Orleans: Tulane University.

Chopin, Kate. (1991). *A Vocation and A Voice*. Intro. By Emily Toth. New York: Penguin Books.

_____. (1970). *The Awakening and Other Stories*. Intro. By Lewis Leary. New York: Holt, Rinehart & Winston, Inc.

Cowan, Walter, Chase, John, Dufour, Charles, LeBlanc, O.K., & Wilds, John. *New Orleans Yesterday and Today*. Baton Rouge: Louisiana State University Press.

Kane, Harnett T. (1949). *Queen New Orleans*. New York: William Morrow & Company.

LeBlanc, Guy. (1996). *Irreverent Guides—New Orleans*. New York: Simon and Schuster, Inc.

Longstreet, Stephen. (1965). *Sportin' House*. Los Angeles: Sherbourne Press, Inc.

Saxon, Lyle. (1928). *Fabulous New Orleans*. New York: D. Appleton-Century Company Incorporated.

Stall, Gaspar J. "Buddy." (1984). *New Orleans: The Inside Story*. Bashing Division.

_____. (1995). *Buddy Stall's Crescent City*. N.p.

Widmer, Mary Lou. (1996). *Margaret Friend of Orphans*. Gretna, LA: Pelican Publishing Company, Inc.

Williams, Tennessee. (1947). *A Streetcar Named Desire*. Norfolk, CT: New Directions Books.

Zenfell, Martha Ellen (Ed.). (1996). *Insight Guides: New Orleans*. London: APA Publications (HK) Ltd.

Index

Other books from Seaside Press

Exploring Branson: A Family Guide

W.C. Jameson

Jameson explores the music scene in Branson, the surrounding countryside, and local tourist attractions.

296 pages • 1-55622-570-9 • $18.95

Exploring Dallas with Children

A Guide for Family Activities (2nd Ed.)

Kay McCasland Threadgill

Exploring Dallas with Children is a complete guide to the fascinating places and unique activities that make the Metroplex the perfect place for family fun.

320 pages • 1-55622-617-9 • $18.95

Exploring San Antonio with Children
A Guide for Family Activities

Docia Schultz Williams

Everything a family needs to know about the many activities found in the Alamo City including festivals and special events, places to go, sports and recreation, performing arts, museums, and more.

320 pages • 1-55622-615-2 • $18.95

Exploring Texas with Children

Sharry Buckner

Information about interesting places in every corner of Texas, especially the lesser known attractions and things to do. A trip planner with phone numbers, directions, and other details.

200 pages • 1-55622-624-1 • $18.95

and Republic of Texas Press

Making it Easy: Southwest Desserts

Chef Pete Nolasco

Great desserts from all over the Southwest to create sensational endings for every kind of meal. Simple, clear instructions and cooking hints and tips from the chef.

200 pages • 1-55622-650-0 • $18.95

Top Texas Chefs Cook at Home: Favorite Entrees

Ginnie Siena Bivona

A showcase of the favorite home cooking recipes of some of the most talented chefs in the state. Each chapter features a story about the chef, his or her life outside the restaurant, hobbies and interests, as well as favorite recipes they use for entertaining in their own homes.

200 pages • 1-55622-651-9 • $18.95

Making it Easy: Cajun Cooking

Chef Arlene Coco

Now the secrets of a longtime Louisiana chef are revealed, and among the recipes are family stories of a time when life on the bayou was sweet and simple.

200 pages • 1-55622-649-7 • $18.95

Popular Seaside Press and Republic of Texas Press Titles

Alamo Movies

At Least 1836 Things You Ought to Know About Texas But Probably Don't

Battlefields of Texas

Best Tales of Texas Ghosts

Bubba Speak: Texas Folk Sayings

A Cowboy of the Pecos

Critter Chronicles

Dallas Uncovered (2nd Edition)

Daughter of Fortune: The Bettie Brown Story

Defense of a Legend

Dirty Dining

Etta Place: Her Life and Times with Butch Cassidy and the Sundance Kid

Exotic Pets: A Veterinary Guide for Owners

Exploring Branson: A Family Guide

Exploring Dallas with Children (2nd Edition)

Exploring New Orleans: A Family Guide

Exploring San Antonio with Children

Exploring Texas with Children

Exploring the Alamo Legends

Eyewitness to the Alamo

First in the Lone Star State

Fixin' to Be Texan

The Funny Side of Texas

Ghosts Along the Texas Coast

The Great Texas Airship Mystery

Horses and Horse Sense

Jackson Hole Uncovered

The Last of the Old-Time Cowboys

Letters Home: A Soldier's Legacy

Los Angeles Uncovered

Making it Easy: Cajun Cooking

Making it Easy: Southwest Desserts

Phantoms of the Plains

Rainy Days in Texas Funbook

Red River Women

Return of Assassin John Wilkes Booth

Return of the Outlaw Billy the Kid

Salt Lake City Uncovered

San Francisco Uncovered

Seattle Uncovered

Spindletop Unwound

Spirits of San Antonio and South Texas

Tales of the Guadalupe Mountains

The Texas Golf Guide

Texas Highway Humor

Texas Ranger Tales

Texas Ranger Tales II

Texas Tales Your Teacher Never Told You

Texas Wit and Wisdom

That Cat Won't Flush

They Don't Have to Die

This Dog'll Hunt

Top Texas Chefs Cook at Home: Favorite Entrees

Trail Rider's Guide to Texas

Treasury of Texas Trivia

Tucson Uncovered

Twin Cities Uncovered

Unsolved Mysteries of the Old West

Unsolved Texas Mysteries

When Darkness Falls

Wild Camp Tales

Your Kitten's First Year

Your Puppy's First Year